Critical Approaches to *Anthills of the Savannah*

D1727101

Impressum

General Editors: Holger G. Ehling, Frank Schulze-Engler, Geoffrey V. Davis.
Editorial Board: Hanno Egner, Marlies Glaser, Ulrike Jamin, Marion Pausch,
Andrea Pohl, Barbara Stute, Monika Trebert.
Board of Advisors: Catherine Acholonu (Owerri), Anne Adams (Ithaca),
Wolfgang Bender (Mainz), Eckhard Breitinger (Bayreuth), Willfried F. Feuser
(Port Harcourt), Raoul Granqvist (Umeå), Jürgen Jansen (Aachen), Reinhard
Küsgen (Göttingen), Jürgen Martini (Bayreuth), Henning Melber (Kassel),
Dieter Riemenschneider (Frankfurt a.M.), Amadou Booker Sadji (Dakar),
Joachim Schultz (Bayreuth), John A. Stotesbury (Joensuu), Peter O. Stummer
(München), Ahmed Yerima (Zaria).
Editor's address: Matatu, In der Au 33, D-6000 Frankfurt a.M. 90.
All correspondence in editorial matters, manuscripts, and books for review
should be sent to the editor. Matatu invites scholarly contributions as well as
creative writing. Manuscripts may be submitted in English or French and
should conform to the MLA-Handbook. Articles should be accompanied by a
brief summary (10-15 lines). Whenever possible, texts should be submitted on
diskette (5¼", IBM-compatible, Word 5.0).
Frequency: Matatu is published twice yearly with approx. 160 pages per issue.
Subscriptions and orders for back issues: To be sent to the publisher's address.
Publisher's address: Editions Rodopi B.V., Keizersgracht 302-304, NL-1016
EX Amsterdam.
Texts published in Matatu are abstracted and indexed in: ACOLIT-Newsletter,
African Literature Association-Bulletin, Bollettino Bibliographico Africano,
Documentatieblad, Internationale Bibliographie der Zeitschriftenliteratur,
Internationale Bibliographie der Rezensionen, Journal of Commonwealth
Literature Annual Bibliography, MLA International Bibliography of Books and
Articles on the Modern Languages and Literatures, The Year's Work in
English Studies.

# Critical Approaches
# to *Anthills of the Savannah*

**ed. Holger G. Ehling**

Amsterdam - Atlanta, GA 1991

# Matatu  Number 8

Front cover: Song of Sorrow, by Obiora Udechukwu

ISBN: 90-5183-318-0
©Editions Rodopi B.V., Amsterdam - Atlanta, GA 1991
Printed in The Netherlands

# Contents - Table des matières

## Poems - Poèmes

## Conference Report

## Book Reviews - Critiques

**Drawings - Illustrations**

The editor wishes to thank Mr. Norbert Aas of Bumerang Press, Bayreuth, for permission to reprint sketches by Obiora Udechukwu, published in What the Madman Said, in this issue of Matatu.

# INTRODUCTION

## CRITICAL APPROACHES TO
## *ANTHILLS OF THE SAVANNAH*

Chinua Achebe is Africa's most popular writer, his works having the highest sales of all African literature. They are considered to be at the very beginning of modern African literatures. Most African authors have in one way or another been influenced by Achebe's writings, and he provided them with a model to deal with language and politics in social setting that was - and still is - changing rapidly.

Since the publication of *A Man of the People* (1966), Achebe's readers had been waiting for another novel - they had to be patient for more than 20 years. 1987, at last, saw the publication of *Anthills of the Savannah*, and critical acclaim was showered on the novel. No doubt, *Anthills of the Savannah* was the most important novel to come out of Africa in the Eighties. It comprises the sum total of Achebe's political and literary thinking as well as of his attempts to come to terms with Nigerian politics and society; here we find new modes of thought, new patterns of discourse.

This is why the editors of *Matatu* thought it worthwhile to devote this issue of *Matatu* entirely to *Anthills of the Savannah*. It is not designed to be an uncritical celebration of the novel. Most authors in this collection appreciate the qualities of Achebe's writing, at the same time pronouncing their criticism.

In his essay, David Maughan Brown argues that Achebe's concept of power is based on naïve and populistic political thinking. He claims that *Anthills of the Savannah* is informed by an ideology of leadership which makes rule of the masses by an elightened élite the only desirable political solution. He finds that the novel contains little trace of the commitment to democracy, let alone the radical populism, of Achebe's extra-fictional statements.

In his article, Ezenwa-Ohaeto states that *Anthills of the Savannah* is representative of Nigerian writing in so far as it reflects the changing preoccupation from criticism of colonialism to criticism of the contemporary political system.

Omar Sougou interprets the novel as being Achebe's answer to criticism of his political views, and to feminist-oriented criticism. Patricia Alden and Chimalum Nwankwo focus on the role of Beatrice, the first woman in an Achebe-novel to be placed in a central position. Both dismiss the point made by enthusiastic critics that this means a shift in Achebe's position on the issue of women in society. Alden, in comparing *Anthills of the Savannah* to Nuruddin Farah's *Sardines*, shows that other writers have gone much further than Achebe.

Raoul Granqvist gives an example of the reception of Achebe's novel in a cultural context informed by Western/Northern preoccupations. The Scandinavian reception of Achebe's novel seems to be typical for the fate of African literatures in European countries whose colonial ties with Africa were only losely knit. And, for German readers, it might be noteworthy that the novel has not yet been published in German - although a translation has been commissioned and completed more than a year ago.

As usual, these essays in *Matatu* are complemented by reviews, reports and creative writing.

*Holger G. Ehling*

*David A. Maughan Brown*

# ANTHILLS OF THE SAVANNAH: ACHEBE'S SOLUTIONS TO THE "TROUBLE WITH NIGERIA"

As an index of their assumptions about their markets, publishers' blurbs often bear examination. The publishers' contribution to the back-cover blurb on the paperback edition of Anthills of the Savannah[1] consists, un-usually, of a single, wholly unexceptionable, sentence: "Chinua Achebe's new novel, his first for 21 years, has been received with great acclaim." The acclaim took the novel as far as the 1987 Booker Prize shortlist. The rest of the blurb consists simply of enthusiastic quotations from reviews. The message is clear: Achebe is so well known that there is no need for biographical notes; this novel has been 21 years in the gestation and critics, as one might expect, have recognised the greatness of so long-awaited a novel from so fine an author.

Achebe was not, of course, silent during those 21 years. Apart from writing poems and short stories, he lectured extensively, published a variety of essays and was generous in granting interviews. A survey of assertions made by Achebe in publications under the last two heads reveals a tendency towards radical populism and an unswerving conviction as to the necessity for "commitment" on the part of writers of fiction. Thus, for example, one finds him asserting that "the masses own the nation because they have the numbers"[2] and declaring:

> These are the real victims of our callous system, the wretched of the earth. They are largely silent and invisible. They don't appear on front pages; they do not initiate industrial actions. They drink bad water and suffer from all kinds of preventable diseases [...] The politician may pay them a siren-visit once in four years and

---

1 Chinua Achebe: *Anthills of the Savannah*. (London: Heinemann, 1987). All references in the text are to this edition.

2 Chinua Achebe: *The Trouble with Nigeria*. (London: Heinemann, 1983), p. 25.

promise to give them this, that and the other. He never says that
what he gives is theirs in the first place.[3]

The wretched of the earth are those who have been
dispossessed. In his use of Fanon, and his endorsement of "the
African revolution", such examples of Achebe's political
commentary in the 1970s and 1980s sound more like the Ngugi of
the 1970s than the Achebe of the 1960s. As early as 1970 we find
Achebe asserting:

> ... the regenerative powers of the people [...] are manifest today
> in the African revolution, a revolution that aims toward true
> independence, that moves toward the creation of modern states in
> place of the new colonial enclaves we have today, a revolution
> that is informed with African ideologies.[4]

Political commentary of this tenor was accompanied in the
same period by comments on the role of the artist which went far
beyond Achebe's often-quoted comments on "The Novelist as
Teacher"[5] and made it clear that when the long-awaited fifth
novel did appear it would be likely to propose socio-political
solutions for what Achebe identified as Nigeria's most serious
problems. One finds Achebe asserting in 1968, "...this is what
literature in Africa should be about today - right and just
causes",[6] and four years later he is saying: "I have come to the
view that you cannot separate the creativity from the revolution
that is inevitable in Africa".[7] Achebe claims for the writer a role
more active, and thereby presumably more influential, than that
of a mere reporter: "...the writer's role is more in determining

---

3  *Ibid.*, p. 24.
4  quoted in Kolawole Ogungbesan: "Politics and the African Writer". *Critical
   Perspectives on Chinua Achebe*. eds. C.L. Innes/Bernth Lindfors
   (Washington, 1978 ), p. 41.
5  Chinua Achebe: *Morning Yet on Creation Day*. (London, 1975).
6  quoted in Ogungbesan, *op. cit.*, p. 40.
7  Ernest and Pat Emenyonu: "Achebe: Accountable to Our Society." *Africa
   Report* 17 (1972), p. 25.

than merely in reporting. In other words his role is to act rather than to react".[8]

This apparent shift in stance with regard to the role of the artist triggered off alarms in critics who subscribed to traditionalist aesthetics predicated on a rigid distinction between "creative writing" and "propaganda". Ogungbesan's response, for example, sounds like a pre-recorded loud-hailer warning directed at anyone venturing too close to the fence:

> The mood of anger, frustration, and despair which Achebe has demonstrated since 1965 [...] constitutes a serious danger to art. Righteous political indignation as the primary impetus for writing belongs more to the world of propaganda than to creative literature. In the writer, it accentuates the personal impulse to write protest and militates against detachment.[9]

When we come to examine Anthills of the Savannah we find, as the comments quoted earlier would lead us to expect, that Achebe stakes a large claim on behalf of the writer of fiction, here wearing the mantle of the story-teller. The Old Man of Abazon, a character for whom the reader's wholly unqualified approval is solicited - partly through the ascription to him of supreme facility both in the use of proverbs and in the art of story-telling - awards the eagle-feather to the story-teller rather than the warrior or the beater of the battle-drum:

> The sounding of the battle-drum is important; the fierce waging of the war itself is important; and the telling of the story afterwards - each is important in its own way. But if you ask me which of them takes the eagle-feather I will say boldly: the story.... Because it is only the story can continue beyond the war and the warrior. It is the story that outlives the sound of war-drums and the exploits of brave fighters. It is the story, not the others, that saves our progeny from blundering like blind beggars into the spikes of the cactus fence. The story is our escort; without it, we are blind. (p.124)

---

8  quoted in Ogungbesan, *op. cit.*, p. 40.
9  *Ibid.*, p. 44.

Setting the story-teller beside the battle-drummer and the warrior is not, of course, as philosophically abstract and allegorical a comparison in post-Biafran Nigeria as it might be elsewhere.

In 1983 Achebe published a booklet outlining what he saw as The Trouble with Nigeria. Interviewed after the publication of Anthills of the Savannah, Achebe made it clear that one of his intentions in the novel had been to take up issues raised in The Trouble with Nigeria and to use his novel to propose solutions. What will save Nigeria's future progeny from blundering like blind beggars into the spikes of the cactus fence is, for Achebe, perhaps obviously enough, better leadership. Achebe's interviewer, Anna Rutherford, says:

> I had the feeling that what you were suggesting was that the society reflected the quality of the leadership; if the leadership was corrupt, the society would also then turn to corruption - in other words, the negative aspects in the society could be directly related back to the negative aspects of the leadership.[10]

Achebe agrees with this interpretation but adds:

> ... but what I'm really interested in is how you could begin to solve this problem. If you're going to do that, you have to pinpoint the responsibility specifically before you can even begin to break out of the vicious circle. And it is at the level of the leadership that this break must occur.[11]

Anthills of the Savannah sets out to solve a problem, and makes large claims for the authority of story-tellers in so doing. My intention in this article is to examine, through an analysis of the novel which is more interested in symptomatic readings than purely aesthetic evaluations, the kind of solution proffered, the extent to which it relates to Achebe's non-fictional assertions about the African "masses" and revolution, and the novel's potential for "determining" the course of Nigerian history rather

---

10 Anna Rutherford: "Interview with Achebe". *Kunapipi* 9.2 (1987), p. 2.
11 *Ibid.*

than merely reporting it. The terms of the evaluation will, then, have been set largely by Achebe's own extra-fictional assertions, particularly with respect to the role of the writer.

Where reception is concerned, my interest here is in the potential effects - in terms of ideological reinforcement or challenge - this novel is likely to have as a conscious intervention in current Nigerian, and more broadly third world, political debate. If the author's role is claimed to be determining, it is obviously legitimate to attempt to assess what political responses the novel is likely to determine. This means that other dimensions of the novel, such, for example, as the symbolic or mythopoeic roles and relationships of the three main characters, pointed to by Fiona Sparrow,[12] will not be looked at. The representative status of the characters in terms of Igbo mythology would only be relevant to my concerns if, for example, Beatrice's role as priestess were to make a significant contribution to the novel's examination of political leadership and thereby shed light on the ideology of leadership informing the novel. I am not convinced that the symbolic or mythological resonance of the characters imparts any greater coherence to the novel's political analysis. Moreover that resonance will be apparent only to a very limited sector of Achebe's readership - those Nigerians well-versed in Igbo mythology and others with a scholarly interest in that mythology - and it cannot, therefore, be regarded as a factor likely to be "determining" where the ideological effect of the novel on the majority of its readers is concerned.

Analysis of the ideological thrust of a political novel will have three main focuses: the content of the message; the characters and characterization employed by the author in conveying that message; and the ways in which the action of the plot is made to demonstrate the essential points of the author's thesis. I will concentrate here on the use Achebe makes of Ikem as the primary vehicle for his message, and the ideology of leadership and reform, rather than revolution, in whose service Ikem lives and dies as a fictional character.

---

12 Sparrow, Fiona: "Review of Anthills of the Savannah." *World Literature Written in English* 28.1 (1988).

Achebe uses various devices for distancing himself as author from Ikem. The two most obvious ones are the criticism, generally very mild, which Ikem comes in for from the other characters - most notable here is Beatrice's criticism of his attitude to women (p.65). Secondly, and potentially rather more tellingly, there is the the omniscient narrator's comment:

> By nature he is never on the same side as his audience. Whatever his audience is, he must try not to be. If they fancy themselves radical, he fancies himself conservative; if they propound right-wing tenets he unleashes revolution. (p.154)

This would suggest that Ikem's adherence to any political position can never be taken at face value, and might seem to serve as insurance against the possibility of his being identified as an authorial spokesperson. But it is, nevertheless, Ikem who is made responsible for expounding the central tenets of the political philosophy on which Achebe's central message about leadership is hung, firstly in the "strange love-letter" (pp. 97-101) he reads to Beatrice - in which he, on the theoretical level at any rate, redeems himself in the face of Beatrice's criticism of his male chauvinism - and, secondly, in his seminal speech at the students' union (pp.152-161).

Ikem's credentials as an authorial voice - if one is listening for an endorsement of the kind of view identified earlier - are established so clearly, in a variety of different ways, that the distancing devices carry very little conviction. Beatrice, who can be taken as a reliable witness throughout, describes Ikem's treatment of women as "about the only chink in his revolutionary armour" (p.65). The reader's sympathy is clearly sought for such statements as Ikem's: "While we do our good works let us not forget that the real solution lies in a world in which charity will have become unnecessary" (p.155). Key scenes like the public executions on the beach are described through Ikem's eyes, and Ikem's perceptions are subsequently authorially endorsed in the interview:

> So you find a leader like the editor of the National Gazette setting himself up to correct the situation. It is people like him who must

initiate the action. It cannot be done by the group on the beach who are delirious and obscenely happy and enjoying the execution.[13]

Most importantly, in that it enables Achebe to provide a continuous - favourable - assessment of Ikem's performance in the crucial speech to the students, he develops a device whereby description of the audience response serves as an index to the incisiveness and accuracy of what Ikem is saying. Thus, for example, the statement that "the laughter had died all of a sudden" (p.160) indicates that Ikem has scored a telling point at the students' expense. This is a device which readers first had the opportunity to familiarize themselves with in the wholly uncontentious context of the long speech given by the Old Man of Abazon at the Harmoney Hotel (pp.122-128).

Apart from canvassing support for resistance to "catchy, half-baked orthodoxy" (p.158), "modish radicals" (p.159) and "half-digested radical rhetoric" (p.161), the main burden of Ikem's political message in the novel lies with his elevation of reform over revolution:

> The sweeping, majestic visions of people rising victorious like a tidal wave against their oppressors and transforming their world with theories and slogans into a new heaven and a new earth of brotherhood, justice and freedom are at best grand illusions. [...] Reform may be a dirty word then but it begins to look more and more like the most promising route to success in the real world. (p.99)

This is obviously a far cry from Achebe's earlier endorsement of "a revolution that aims toward true independence" with its apparent recognition that neo-colonialism and mere "flag" independence are no more amenable to "reform" than is apartheid. Rather than simply applauding or castigating Achebe, depending on whether the critic shares the views being expressed by Ikem - Larry Diamond's euphoria over Ikem's "stunning

---

13 Interview, *op. cit.*, p. 2.

oration"[14] appears to be a prime example of critical adulation based on ideological concurrence - one of literary criticism's functions in this context should presumably be to note the disparity between the ideological positions endorsed by the fiction on the one hand and by the extra-fictional statements on the other. This opens up the question as to where the contradiction derives from: whether from a recent historical shift in Achebe's political views or, as with some of Ngugi's early fiction,[15] from an aesthetic ideology which determines that what may be asserted freely outside fiction becomes "propaganda", and therefore illegitimate, in fiction.

The solution proposed by the novel is couched in terms of "leadership", a preoccupation carried over into the fiction from Achebe's non-fictional statements. The first sentence of The Trouble with Nigeria states quite baldly: "The trouble with Nigeria is simply and squarely a failure of leadership".[16] Achebe then comments, "The Nigerian problem is the unwillingness or inability of its leaders to rise to the responsibility, to the challenge of personal example which are the hallmarks of true leadership", and he concludes a few pages later that:

> ... every single day of continued neglect brings [Nigeria] ever closer to the brink of the abyss. To pull her back and turn her around is clearly beyond the contrivance of mediocre leadership. It calls for greatness.[...] Nigerians are what they are only because their leaders are not what they should be.[17]

In 1988 Achebe can be found interpreting the causes of the Biafran war in exactly the same terms: "The war resulted from

14 Larry Diamond: "Fiction as Political Thought." *African Affairs*, (1989), p. 439.
15 David Maughan-Brown: *Land, Freedom and Fiction*. (London, 1985), pp. 247-258.
16 Achebe, Trouble, *op.cit.*, p. 1.
17 *Ibid.*, p. 10.

the failure of the leadership of Nigeria to protect significant portions of the population from a pogrom, from destruction".[18]

In pursuit of this leadership thesis Achebe is prepared to go as far as asserting that "after two decades of bloodshed and military rule" in "one of the most corrupt, insensitive, inefficient places under the sun"[19] what his "society craves today is not a style of leadership which projects and celebrates the violence of power but the sobriety of peace".[20] What the wretched of the earth "crave" as the solution to the "gargantuan disparity of privilege" between the "tiny class" of the elite and "the vast multitudes of ordinary Nigerians"[21] is, we are told, a change in leadership style. Achebe concludes that "if Nigeria is to avoid catastrophes of possibly greater dimensions than we have been through since Independence we must take a hard and unsentimental look at the crucial question of leadership and political power".[22] Leadership and political power constitute a single "question": the possibility is never entertained that there might be a separation of the concept of "political power" from that of "leadership".

When this concern with leadership finds direct expression in Anthills of the Savannah we find reference to "leaders who openly looted our treasury, whose effrontery soiled our national soul" (p.42). Ikem comes to the conclusion that the "prime failure" of leadership in Kangan, the novel's fictionalized version of Nigeria, can be seen as "the failure of our rulers to re-establish vital inner links with the poor and dispossessed of this country, with the bruised heart that throbs painfully at the core of the nation's being" (p.141). Precisely what kind of "vital inner links with the poor" are envisaged, and how they might be re-established, remains unspecified. The closest Achebe could come to a concrete proposal in The Trouble with Nigeria was the less than wholly persuasive suggestion that Shagari, the President of

---

18 Phillip van Niekerk: "Chinua Achebe breaks his silence". *Weekly Mail*, September 8, 1988, p. 14.
19 Achebe, Trouble, *op.cit.*, p. 9.
20 *Ibid.*, p. 34.
21 *Ibid.*, p. 22.
22 *Ibid.*, p. 59.

Nigeria at the time, "should return home, read the papers and from time to time talk to Nigerians outside the circle of the Presidential aides and party faithfuls".[23] Ideally, this would presumably include those very few among the wretched of the earth who would be likely to want to sit down and chat unrestrainedly with the President.

The obsession with "leadership" is so pervasive in Anthills of the Savannah that it intrudes apparently aimlessly in areas where, even taking the mythopoeic dimension of the novel into account, it is very difficult to believe that Achebe is trying to make any significant point. Thus, for example, we are told of Beatrice at the naming ceremony in the final chapter: "She, on her part, was a captain whose leadership was sharpened more and more by sensitivity to the peculiar needs of her company" (p.229). While heightened sensitivity is obviously desirable, one needs to ask what purpose is being served by the terminology of military hierarchy involved in designating Beatrice as a "captain" with a "company" when she is simply entertaining a handful of friends at her home.

It is not necessary to my purposes to take systematic issue with the substance of Ikem's central political arguments in the novel. The thinness of much of the argument is perhaps best illustrated by the false analogy between "society" as "an extension of the individual", rather than a historically determined structure of individual and class relationships, on the one hand, and the individual psyche, on the other, whereby it is argued that because doing more than "re-forming" the individual psyche would be "overthrowing" it and "unleashing insanity" it therefore follows that: "It has to be the same with society. You re-form it around what it is, its core of reality; not around an intellectual abstraction" (p.100). What this apparently unchanging "core of reality" of "society" is, remains, once again, unspecified - but it would appear, from what has already been said, to include a historically unchanging division of humanity into the "leaders" and the led.

---

23 *Ibid.*, p. 38.

What I am primarily interested in here is, rather, the identification of tensions and contradictions in Anthills of the Savannah resulting from Achebe's attempt to use the novel as a vehicle for proposing solutions to the socio-political and economic problems of Nigeria. It may, apart from anything else, prove instructive to an understanding of the political culture determining the contemporary reception of African Literatures to attempt to establish the political co-ordinates of a novel so enthusiastically received by most western reviewers. The novel is the fictional product of 21 years of political experience and contemplation on the part of a highly, and deservedly, respected author convinced of the functional obligations of literature and of the writer's duty to teach and lead his or her people, and accordingly it must invite analysis in these terms. One might, however, be forgiven for suspecting that the novel attempts to pre-empt this kind of scrutiny: "In the vocabulary of certain radical theorists contradictions are given the status of some deadly disease to which their opponents alone can succumb" (p.100).

"Contradictions" should be seen as belonging to the vocabulary of analysis rather than invective. They derive unavoidably from the conflicting determinations acting on an author: from, for example, the discrepancies between the events of history and conflicting class-based readings of those events; from anxieties about the role of the intellectual and artist in oppositional and, in particular, revolutionary politics; from a discordance between the class-based ideological perspectives of writers and their assumptions about the perspectives of their putative audiences; from the tensions between the content of the message to be conveyed and the aesthetic demands of the form being used. It is one of the functions of criticism to attempt to identify and account for tensions and contradictions in an author's work, particularly where they are likely to determine the ideological effects of the work on its readers.

Contradictions and confusions can be discerned at all levels in Anthills of the Savannah, from the fictional devices used through to the solutions being proposed. Thus, at the simple level, the device of using the assembled students' responses as the index of Ikem's unanswerable incisiveness is seriously weakened

by the students' being made to be highly sensitive and reliable
sounding-boards one moment and immature adolescents in dire
need of Ikem's political hectoring the next. The assembled
students are described as a "ticklishly humorous crowd" (p.156)
whose applause, "redoubled laughter" (p.160), "explosion of
laughter" (p.160), "mixed noises" (p.159) and "uproarious
laughter" (p.161) Ikem can manipulate at will. So anxious is
Achebe to involve the reader in the process of educating the
students, whose responses are observed from Ikem's position of
lofty detachment behind the lectern, that he is even betrayed into
a direct, albeit single-worded, address to the reader: "Tremendous
applause. Surprisingly?" (p.161) The students come across during
the time for questions after the lecture as a bunch of politically
naive and unthinking buffoons who are out for a laugh. Yet this is
the same audience which was used earlier as the sounding-board
for a speech (p.153) "so well crafted and so powerfully spoken it
took on the nature and scope of an epic prose-poem", which is
apparently deemed sufficient reason for Achebe's not having to
confront the difficulty of providing, or even summarising, the
content of the speech. The same audience, which needs to be told
"not to swallow every piece of superstition you are told by witch
doctors [sic] and professors" (p.161), which is apparently prone
to "too much parroting, too much regurgitating of half-digested
radical rhetoric" (p.161), is said to have "sat or stood silently
entranced" (p.154) in appreciation of the epic prose-poem.

The one area in which the students show themselves to be
manifestly inadequate when it comes to political discourse -
though it is clearly not Achebe's intention to make them seem so -
is in the recognition of a use of the terminology of class analysis
by the speakers from the platform, including Ikem, which is so
hopelessly imprecise as to render that terminology entirely useless
for any analytical purposes whatever, irrespective of whether the
preferred paradigm is liberal or marxist. So, for example, one
finds the sudden creation of "students as a class", in other than
the class-room sense, from Ikem (p.160); we are encouraged to
believe that workers cease to be members of the working class if
they happen to be lazy (p.160); the students (and Ikem) accept the
definition of "the proletariat" as "peasants, workers and students"

(p.156); and we are told, again by Ikem, that a market woman "qualifies along with peasants for a seat among the proletariat" (p.157). By the time the reader arrives at an account of the police beating female students, an episode identified by the omniscient narrator as the "compounding [of] an ancient sex-feud with today's war of the classes" (p.173), it is impossible to know precisely what "classes" the narrator, and presumably Achebe, thinks he is referring to.

Ikem's concluding injunction, towards which the whole speech to the students leads, is itself contradictory, given Achebe's ascription of all responsibility for social ills to "leaders". Ikem tells the students:

> I have no desire to belittle your role in putting this nation finally on the road to self-redemption. But you cannot do that unless you first set about to purge yourselves, to clean up your act. You must learn for a start to hold your own student leaders to responsible performance; only after you have done that can you have the moral authority to lecture the national leadership. (p.160)

This confuses matters considerably. If so heavy a weight of responsibility lies with the leaders, it cannot also lie with the led. The whole leadership thesis obviously falls down if it is the responsibility of those who are led to "hold ... [their] leaders to responsible performance" - irresponsible performance then becomes the responsibility of those who failed to keep an adequate hold on their leaders.

The novel's concluding message, as explicated in the interview by Achebe, seems equally contradictory:

> I think this group around Beatrice has learnt a lot in the course of the story. They have learnt, for instance, that the little clique that saw themselves as leaders was not big enough, that it had no perception of incorporating others. You have to incorporate the taxi drivers, the market women, the peasants, the workers, the students. You have to broaden out so that when you are talking

you are talking for the people, you are not only talking for a section or a group interest.[24]

What is needed is not a little clique of leaders but a big clique of leaders; the group must broaden out to enable it to talk "for the people", who, crucially, are still presumed to be unable to talk for themselves. But as you broaden out how do you retain your concept of "leadership"? If, as Achebe maintains, the role of leadership is "to create the circumstances in which the people begin to act with awareness"[25] do the incorporated taxi drivers, market women and peasants then represent the "people" beginning to act with awareness, or are they now "leaders"? It would seem from the distinction Achebe draws elsewhere between the "elite" and the "people" that leadership is probably, in fact, the preserve of the elite: "The elite are important because they have been given special training and education and qualifications and their duty is to use it to initiate the upward movement of the people".[26] But it is awkward, at the very least, for a political analysis so totally dependent on a concept of "leadership" to have the boundary between the leaders and the led becoming so blurred.

There are times in the novel when the insistence on "leadership" comes across as a reflex, almost rote, response. Here the reflections are Chris's, but there is no reason whatever to imagine that Achebe is in any way distancing himself from what is being said:

> And to think of it, that imaginative roadside welder who created the first crude buses might be the managing director of the transport company that now had a fleet of Luxuriouses! If there had been no progress in the nation's affairs at the top there had clearly been some near the bottom, albeit undirected and therefore only half-realized. (p.201)

---

24 Interview, *op. cit.*, p. 3.
25 *Ibid.*
26 *Ibid.*, p. 5.

There can be no real progress without "leadership". What appears as progress without benefit of "leadership" and "direction" can, at best, only be "half-realized". Here the belated genuflection in the direction of "leadership" leads to absurdity: would the only "half-realized" progress of the roadside welder have resulted, had it been "directed", in his somehow miraculously being duplicated into two managing directors? Or is Chris wrong in speculating that he might be managing director - without "direction" is the limit of his capability only to become half a managing director, perhaps personal assistant to the managing director?

Outside the fiction, Achebe's fixation on "leadership" leads to a (probably absent-minded) denial of history which contradicts the stress on history of such comments as: "The most meaningful work that African writers can do today will take into account our whole history: how we got here, and what it is today; and this will help us to map our plans for the future".[27] Thus we find Achebe asserting that "in traditional African society, there is a distinct division between the poet and the emperor"[28] and remarking that "the lack of real leaders in Igboland goes back, of course, to the beginnings of colonial administration".[29] Where "traditional African society" in Igboland is concerned, Achebe is obviously fully aware that emperors were an unknown phenomenon; nor were there "real leaders" in the political sense in which the term is used by Achebe - members of a ruling elite - in Igboland prior to the beginnings of colonial administration, any more than there were after those beginnings. The assumption of "rule", taken for granted as the obvious and inevitable way of ordering society, an assumption which permeates Achebe's political commentary, leads to further implicit denials of pre-colonial Igbo history (where political decision-making was far more democratic than this concept of "rule" would allow) as, for example, in such observations as: "True patriotism is possible only when the people who rule and those under their power have

---

27 Emenyonu, *op.cit.*, p. 25.
28 van Niekerk, *op.cit.*, 14.
29 Achebe, *Trouble*, p. 48.

a common and genuine goal of maintaining the dispensation under which the nation lives".[30]

For all Achebe's avowed populist sympathy for "the wretched of the earth", and his recognition that when politicians give hand-outs to the people what they are "giving" the people already, in fact, belongs to the people, some of Achebe's formulations give rise to the suspicion that the fixation with "leadership" might, in fact, derive from an underlying contempt - though "contempt" is probably too strong a term - for "the people". Thus, for example, one finds Achebe asserting, in the context of manifestly vicious, incompetent and corrupt leaders, that "the people get the leadership they deserve up to a point".[31] More tellingly, he denies "the people" any capacity to think: "leaders" are defined by virtue of their being "the few thinking people".[32] This translates in Anthills of the Savannah into Ikem's, apparently authorially endorsed, reflections on the taxi-drivers:

> The elation came perhaps from this rare human contact across station and class with these two who had every cause to feel hatred but came instead with friendship, acting out spontaneously and without self-righteousness what their betters preach so often but so seldom practise. (p.136)

The use of "betters" in this context is suggestive of so ingrained and perverse a perception of society as being naturally divided along essentially class lines, where class is signalled by education, as to turn language on its head. While, at a superficial level, "betters" carries an element of rather clumsy irony - to give Achebe the benefit of the doubt as to whether the usage isn't simply absent-minded - the whole didactic point of the comment depends on the acceptance of a hierarchy of class distinction. If they aren't inherently "betters" there is no point in dwelling on the inadequacies of their behaviour which undermine their claim to being "betters".

---

30  *Ibid.*, p. 16.
31  Interview, *op. cit.*, p. 2.
32  *Ibid.*

But it is not only Achebe's incidental use of language which raises questions about his underlying attitude to "the people" whose cause he champions. One needs to ask why it is that Achebe chooses as the central scene, representative of the essence of "the people", the public execution on the beach. It isn't adequate to answer: "The fact [is] that the people are prone to this kind of behaviour".[33] The people are also prone to other kinds of behaviour. Ikem, through whose eyes the execution scene is portrayed, is much taken by the Gelegele Market:

> I never pass up a chance of just sitting in my car, reading or pretending to read, surrounded by the vitality and thrill of these dramatic people. Of course the whole of Gelegele Market is one thousand live theatres going at once (p.47).

Yet Achebe does not choose to make any of the thousand live theatres of the Gelegele Market central to his depiction of "the people". That he doesn't do so can be attributed to the fact that the Gelegele Market offers no obvious occasion for demonstrating the need for leadership - which the execution scene, by contrast, clearly does:

> The fact that the people are prone to this kind of behaviour, that they could come to a stage where they could relish this kind of scene, must make the leadership say to itself, "Why is this possible? How can this happen? It is wrong. We must do something about it." So you find a leader like the editor of the National Gazette setting himself up to correct the situation. It is people like him who must initiate the action.[34]

What Ikem, in fact, does is to have the public executions stopped. This is obviously a good thing, but it in no way even begins "to do something about" the prior "fact that the people are prone to this kind of behaviour".

The centrality given to the "delirious and obscenely happy"[35] crowd at the execution scene, however accurate a

---

33  *Ibid.*
34  *Ibid.*
35  *Ibid.*

depiction of such an event the scene may be, is not "natural" or inevitable, it is the product of ideologically determined selection on the part of the author, who had many other options open to him. It is clearly directed towards proving the necessity for "leadership" of the inherently brutish masses by an elite - as Achebe himself asserts: "Stories ... are not innocent".[36] One would clearly not wish to take the analogy any further, but I find it difficult to see any way in which an attempt to portray the mass hysteria of a crowd at a public execution as "typical" of "the people", in the interests of asserting the need for "leadership" by an elite, can be seen to differ in kind from the ideological manipulations involved, for example, in attempts by apologists for white supremacy in South Africa to argue a "necklacing" as "typical" of blacks, and therefore evidence of the need for continued white domination. The specific political ends to which the manipulation of readers' sympathies is being put are obviously worlds apart, but that should not obscure the similarities between the ideological manipulation involved in each case.

Achebe's view of human nature appears to be pessimistic. Ikem is allowed, for example, to reflect: "...I grab my torchlight and take her down our unswept and unlit stairs. Whenever I go up or down those stairs I remember the goat owned in common that dies of hunger" (p.36). Authorial approval of Ikem would appear undismayed by the fact that, as one of the common owners, he presumably bears part of the responsibility for the goat's death. It must be assumed to be this unenthusiastic view of "human nature" that underlies the fundamentally undemocratic tendency of Achebe's obsession with "leadership". Chris's final message in the novel, a message uttered with his dying breath, is interpreted by Beatrice as a declaration that: "This world belongs to the people of the world not to any little caucus, no matter how talented..." (p.232). Yet nowhere in the novel, or in The Trouble with Nigeria, is the possibility ever entertained that "rule" by an elite leadership might be replaced by genuinely democratic structures, whereby the people could become responsible for the government of the world that is said to belong to them. The logic

---

36 *Ibid.*, p. 5.

of Achebe's fixation on "leadership", as embodied in this novel, would lead not to democracy but to enlightened dictatorship by the elite - an outcome somewhat at odds with the populist tendency of some of Achebe's views quoted earlier. Though it is not, of course, at odds with the role claimed for the intellectual, and the writer in particular, through the award of the eagle-feather to the story-teller.

For a writer who aspires to a role that lies "more in determining than merely reporting", what Achebe provides by way of guidance for his society for the future looks a bit thin - rather more so than one might imagine from some of the acclaim with which Anthills of the Savannah has been greeted. We find a surprisingly passive (if also unusually frank) acceptance of impotence as a price one is told one must be prepared to pay for freedom of thought - articulated by the student leader Emmanuel, but derived from Ikem: "...we may accept a limitation on our actions but never, under no circumstances, must we accept restriction on our thinking" (p.223). We find an assertion that the world belongs to the people of the world, but no suggestion as to how those people can become involved in the government of their world. Instead, we are presented with a view of the people sufficiently unflattering for us not to be particularly enthusiastic about encouraging their involvement in government.

We are told that "experience and intelligence warn us that man's progress in freedom will be piecemeal, slow and undramatic" (p.99) but we are given little insight as to what should be demanded of that "freedom". We are shown the unsatisfactory relationships and attitudes of a group of leaders, but this is done in such a way as never to call oligarchical "rule" or "leadership" per se into question. Although the head of state is a military officer who owes his position to a coup, the answer to the problems appears not to lie with political structures but to be a matter of leadership style. We are left entirely in the dark as to how a change in leadership style may be supposed to be able to solve the structural problems inherent in creating out of a society characterised by massive inequalities "a world in which charity will have become unnecessary" (p.155). The recipe for an acceptable leadership style - the re-establishing of "vital inner links ... with the bruised heart that throbs painfully at the core of the nation's being" (p.141) - is less than helpful in its lack of precision and sounds to have more in common with Patience Strong than it has with any recognised theory of Political Science.

The sometimes contradictory and always inherently undemocratic solutions Anthills of the Savannah proposes to the "Trouble with Nigeria" seem to me unlikely, to use Achebe's phrase, to be "determining" - they certainly haven't determined the generally adulatory tenor of the response the novel has met from reviewers. As solutions they carry little conviction and seem unlikely to have the durability of the anthills of the savannah, capable of enduring many seasons of grassfires.

*Ezenwa-Ohaeto*

# PATRIOTS AND PARASITES: THE METAPHOR OF POWER IN ACHEBE'S *ANTHILLS OF THE SAVANNAH*

The reality of contemporary events places much emphasis on the use and misuse of power. This reality is heightened in an acrimonious environment where social, economic and political power are subjected to varied manipulations by miscellaneous groups and communities. This manipulation of power becomes important in the effort to rectify all forms of deviations in the society for:

> ... to possess power or to be powerful is, then, to have a generalized potentiality for getting one's way or for bringing about changes (at least some of which are intended) in other people's actions or conditions.[1]

In Africa the interests of various individuals and groups have transformed the possession of power into nightmarish dimensions due to the flaws in the political structures of the societies. Although some of these degenerative weaknesses have been explained by historical experiences, there still remains the fact that the progressive development of any society depends on a conscious pruning of flaws in the organizational structure of the society by those with the power to provide guidance and direction. Moreover, this burden of leadership could elicit either patriotic or parasitic tendencies in the utilization and exercise of power.

Chinua Achebe, whose novels have artistically explored this issue of power in various dimensions, is aware that power could lead to both progressive objectives and destructive aims. His novels have shown the issues of power at both the communal and individualistic levels. In *Things Fall Apart* he shows the limits of

---

1   Paul Edwards: "Power". *The Encyclopedia of Philosophy*; 6, (New York, 1967), pp. 424-426.

mundane power as it concerns the protagonist within the ambits of cultural power; in *Arrow of God* it is the exploration of divine power; in *No Longer at Ease* it is the analysis of intellectual power, while *A Man of the People* examines political power and its consequences. A thematic link between this last novel and Achebe's recent novel is created through the nature of the subject matter, for *A Man of the People* ends with a coup while *Anthills of the Savannah*[2] explores the consequences of that coup. The reality of coup plotting and military politics involves a forceful disruption and acquisition of power which generates splits in the social structures. I shall therefore examine the metaphor of power in *Anthills of the Savannah* through an analysis of the patriots and parasites that Achebe has created as characters and their interactions.

The issue of power in this novel is presented through the perspectives of four major characters: His Excellency Sam, Christopher Oriko, Ikem Osodi and Beatrice Okoh. However, the centrality of power in the novel is graphically shown through the author's reflection on a myth which one of the communities in the fictitious nation of Kangan has fashioned to explain their reality. The author presents the myth thus:

> In the beginning Power rampaged through our world naked. So the Almighty, looking at his creation through the round undying eye of the sun, saw and pondered and finally decided to send his daughter, Idemili, to bear witness to the moral nature of authority by wrapping around Power's rude waist a loin cloth of peace and modesty (p. 102).

Although this mythology is used by the author to explain the invaluable role of Beatrice, it is a succinct commentary on the limits of personified power. This image of power rampaging "naked" also illustrates the necessity for a conscious control of power and its refinement with moral values. It is this mixture of power with moral values that informs the subsequent exploration of power in *Anthills of the Savannah*.

---

2 Chinua Achebe: *Anthills of the Savannah*. (London and Ibadan: Heinemann, 1987). All references to this edition.

The major character known as His Excellency is a personification of military power in the novel, and his meeting with his Commissioners provides an indication of the use of power at the apex of the societal structure. His Excellency is a supreme executor of power as the character Christopher Oriko highlights when he says that "days are good or bad for us now according to how His Excellency gets out of bed in the morning" (p.2). Where the exercise of power depends on the whims of its wielder without an intelligent appraisal of reality, it leads to a distortion of social values and human lives. However, the sacrosanct nature of this power depends on the willingness of the followers to flatter the ruler. Oriko sarcastically comments on this behaviour:

> I can hear in advance the many compliments we will pay him as soon as his back is turned: that the trouble with His Excellency is that he can never hurt a man and go to sleep over it (p.3).

But this flattery leads the flatterers into destruction: His Excellency not only hurts his best friends but also organizes their murder. The supreme irony which this man who "can never hurt a man and go to sleep over it" illustrates, is the fact that a leader can use his dictatorial powers to prevent even a whole region from receiving its due share of the national resources.

The materialization of His Excellency as a Head of State is used by the author as a metaphor for condemning the freakish accidents that place unprepared, inadequate individuals into positions of power. The first narrator, Christopher Oriko informs us thus:

> His Excellency came to power without any preparation for political leadership - a fact which he being a very intelligent person knew perfectly well and which, furthermore, should not have surprised anyone. Sandhurst after all did not set about training officers to take over Her Majesty's throne but rather in the high tradition of proud aloofness from politics and public affairs. Therefore when our civilian politicians finally got what they had coming to them and landed unloved and unmourned on the rubbish heap and the young Army Commander was invited by

the even younger coup makers to become His Excellency the
Head of State he had pretty few ideas about what to do (p.12).

This issue of unpreparedness and lack of ideas is at the core
of the exercise of power by His Excellency because ignorance
compounds his leadership problems. His subsequent
transformation into a parasite in power means that he could only
generate political excesses. He fails to set himself the task of
changing the social reality of Kangan, thereby encouraging
squalid and vicious squabbles among his followers. Achebe
obviously indicts those who seek power without a corresponding
idea of how to utilize that power.

Nevertheless, His Excellency is aware of the extent of his
power, for it is this awareness which makes his dictatorial
tendencies frightening and unpleasant to both his associates and
the people of Kangan. It has been noted that

> domination may be based upon coercion, authority or influence;
> although they are not mutually exclusive any given hierarchical
> relation is likely to be predominantly coercive, authoritarian or
> influential.[3]

In this instance coercion is the ultimate weapon of His
Excellency who reminds one of his Commissioners: "Attorney-
General, I sent for you not to read me a lecture but to answer my
question. You may be the Attorney but don't forget I am the
General" (p.22). This pun on the word "General" reflects the
attitude of this leader to the possession of power for it shows that
he does not value the legal aspects of power especially when it
concerns the security of his unpopular desire to be President-for-
Life.

The portrayal of the Head of State in this novel thus
becomes a dramatization of Achebe's view that

> ... the trouble with Nigeria is simply and squarely a failure of
> leadership. There is nothing basically wrong with the Nigerian
> land or climate or water or air or anything else. The Nigerian

---

3   Roderick Martin: *The Sociology of Power*. (London, 1977), p. 161.

problem is the unwillingness or inability of its leaders to rise to
the responsibility, to the challenge of personal example which are
the hallmarks of true leadership.[4]

It is the anatomy of this responsibility of leadership which
Achebe achieves through the portrait of His Excellency presiding
over the fictitious and metaphorical country of Kangan.

*Anthills of the Savannah* is about the machinations of power
which Ikem Osodi captures in his "Hymn to the Sun". The sun in
this hymn symbolizes His Excellency and the poet/journalist uses
a mythological story concerning the people of Abazon to
comment on the reluctance of the Head of State to perform his
duties. The drought in Abazon has caused untold hardship "so
they send a deputation of elders to the government who hold the
yam today, and hold the knife, to seek help of them" (p.33).
Although the reference in this poem to the sun is also literal, it is
the symbolic nature of that reference which makes the author's
concern important, for it shows that power could be used to
punish even a community. The lack of concern for the effects of
the drought in Abazon is based on the fact that they did not
endorse His Excellency's desire for a life-presidency.

Ikem Osodi feels that in order to counter this abuse of
power the "best weapon against them is not to marshall facts, of
which they are truly managers, but passion" (p.38). The passion
which Osodi arouses is through his editorials in the National
Gazette which influences certain Government decisions like the
cessation of the persecution of the cynical but efficient Mad
Medico and the clean-up of the Bassa taxipark. However, the
irony which arises through this power of a newspaper is that it is
the same newspaper which publishes the false information that
Ikem Osodi has advocated regicide, thereby accelerating the
actions leading to his arrest and murder by security forces. The
author is clearly indicating that in the use of all variations of
power the wielder must be aware of the varied limitations in order
not to harm society.

---

4   Chinua Achebe: *The Trouble With Nigeria.* (Enugu, 1983), p. 1.

Ikem Osodi is aware of the consequences of power for he uses the aphorism that "power is like marrying across the Niger: you soon find yourself paddling by night". He also comments that

> worshipping a dictator is such a pain in the ass. It wouldn't be so bad if it was merely a matter of dancing upside down on your head. With practice anyone could learn to do that. The real problem is having no way of knowing from one day to another, from one minute to the next, just what is up and what is down (p.45).

The result of this confusion is that the Commissioner for Information, Christopher Oriko becomes the last person to be given the vital information concerning the constant changes of His Excellency's decisions. The confusion highlights the irony of a situation in which a Commissioner for Information is not informed, thereby adding grotesque humour to the ineptitude of power wielders.

The third narrator, Beatrice Okoh, is shown to possess vision and sense especially in her analysis of human nature - quite unlike Oriko and Osodi who are blinded by their legendary altercations. This female character that Chinua Achebe uses to advance the ideas in *Anthills of the Savannah* is obviously a response to the accusations that his "macho spirit with its disdain for women robs him of the symbolic insight into the nurturant possibilities of women's vital role"[5] and also that "while Achebe's works are obvious classics within the African literary tradition, a re-examination of his work from a feminist position reveals woman as peripheral to the larger experience of man's experience".[6]

---

5   Jemi Ogunbiyi (ed.): Chikwenye Okonjo Ogunyemi: "Women and Nigerian Literature". *Perspectives on Nigerian Literature: 1700 to the Present.* (Lagos, 1988), p. 67.

6   Carole Boyce Davies/Anne Adams Graves (ed.): "Motherhood in the Works of Male and Female Igbo Writers: Achebe, Emecheta, Nwapa and Nzekwu". *Ngambika: Studies of Women in African Literature.* (Trenton, NJ, 1986), p. 247.

The character of Beatrice therefore takes into considerations these negative observations concerning his creativity for she not only functions as a recognizable active individual, but also as an ameliorating influence on the use of power. Her relationship with the three major characters, His Excellency, Chris Oriko and Ikem Osodi, thus becomes symbolic of the feminine element which must complement the masculine essence of power that Achebe captures in the myth of Idemili referred to earlier in this study.

The importance of Beatrice is realised through her desire to turn the three men functioning as Head of State, Commissioner and Editor respectively, towards a sensitive appreciation of the sutble nuances of life. Beatrice is aware of her duty in the society.

> I was determined from the very beginning to put my career first and, if need be, last. That every woman wants a man to complete her is a piece of male chauvinist bullshit I had completely rejected before I knew there was anything like women's lib (p.188).

This determination to make the career the centre of consciousness in her life does not isolate Beatrice from the emotional aspect of reality for she becomes the girlfriend of Christopher Oriko. It is this relationship between Beatrice and the three men where she functions as Oriko's girl friend, Ikem Osodi's sisterly friend and His Excellency's friendly patriot, which magnifies the dimensions of power that Achebe portrays in the novel.

Beatrice inspires Ikem Osodi to re-think his perception of womanhood for he acknowledges that, "the women are, of course, the biggest single group of oppressed people in the world and, if we are to believe the Book of Genesis, the very oldest" (p.98), and his solution is that in the effort to tame the power that has been wielded to oppress women, the society has to be reformed but "you re-form it around what it is, its core of reality; not around an intellectual abstraction" (p.100). Ikem Osodi's recognition that the status of women in society has to be reformed, indicates the emphasis which Achebe has now placed on womanhood that has an onerous task to perform in the refinement of power channelled towards the development of the society.

Despite Beatrice's success in inspiring Ikem Osodi, she fails to create the same impression on His Excellency. The utilization of her female charms to redirect His Excellency towards acknowledging that a leader is responsible for making positive changes in society is unsuccessful. When she asks His Excellency with calm logic

> If I went to America today, to Washington DC, would I, could I, walk into a White House private dinner and take the American President hostage. And his Defence Chief and his Director of CIA? (p.81),

she is dismissed as a racist.

This is one of the fatal blows to the positive use of power by Beatrice, and this impossibility to penetrate the insensitive mind of His Excellency causes the subsequent avoidable disasters. Achebe illustrates, through this incident, that the positive exercise of power depends on the motives of the wielder, and that in the case of Beatrice she possesses what "Ikem alone came close to sensing" which is the power of

> ...the village priestess who will prophesy when her divinity rides her abandoning if need be her soup-pot on the fire, but returning again when the god departs to the domesticity of kitchen or the bargaining market-stool behind her little display of peppers and dry fish and green vegetables (p.105).

The power which Beatrice would exercise in this case has divine implications and she sees it as a duty to act towards an elimination of the flaws in the social structures through a pruning of the excesses of those individuals in positions of authority. This responsibility makes her insist that the differences of opinion in strategies and tactics ought not to undermine fatally the object of the struggle.

There is a juxtaposition of Beatrice with other women which reflects her special position in the hierarchy of social importance and responsibility. Beatrice recognizes this special position for she tells Chris:

> ... you called me a priestess. No, a prophetess, I think. I mind only the Cherubim and Seraphim part of it. As a matter of fact, I do sometimes feel like Chielo in the novel, the priestess and prophetess of the Hills and the Caves (p.114).

It is therefore not surprising that Beatrice perceives reality from a higher angle which enables her to exhibit humane qualities through her economic power. Achebe places her humanity beside the insensitivity of Agatha, who "... was so free with leaflets dripping with the saving blood of Jesus and yet had no single drop of charity in her own anaemic blood" (p.183). The idea which Achebe makes persuasive here is that the use of labels to create an aura of virtue does not obliterate the basic nature of the individual, for Beatrice does not require stimulants like religion in order to be kind, loyal and honest to the ordinary people in the society.

Power is not only exercised by the four major characters in this novel - the numerous minor characters in their social interactions wield varied forms of power. The author shows one of these variations of power through the old man who led the delegation from Abazon to plead for the provision of the basic necessities of life for his people, especially water. This man uses the power of his words to cast insight on the responsibility that must be associated with power. When he comments that

> ... to some of us the owner of the world has apportioned the gift to tell their fellows that the time to get up has finally come. To others He gives the eagerness to rise when they hear the call to rise with racing blood and put on their garbs of war and go to the boundary of their town to engage the invading enemy boldly in battle. And then there are those others whose part is to wait and when the struggle is ended, to take over and recount its story (p.123),

he is making clear the various available levels of power. The substance of this old man's speech becomes sorrowful when he concludes that they have come to the Big Chief to say "our own yes and perhaps the work on our bore-holes will start again and we will not all perish from the anger of the sun" (p.127). This reference to the sun becomes both a symbol and a metonymy for the destructive power associated with rulers like His Excellency.

The artistic exploration of power in *Anthills of the Savannah* also emerges through Achebe's ability to present its various levels based on social and economic circumstances. Achebe delves into power at the lowest level of society in order to illustrate that the misuse of power is not restricted to those at the apex. The soldiers, even at the level where they are not officers, betray tendencies to misuse power. The soldier-driver who nearly kills a young man abuses him: "If I kill you I kill dog" (p.48). The soldier who searches Beatrice's home is rude, brutal and wicked. In his lack of consideration this red-eyed Sergeant pulled "out the bedsheets off the bed and [threw] them on the floor where he walked all over them as he frenziedly darted from one object to another" (p.177). Furthermore the policeman who arrests Ikem Osodi for the flimsy reason that he failed to put on his parking light in a well lit environment is rude. Despite the characteristic Achebe-humour, this scene is tragic for it shows the ignorance of law enforcement agents. The dialogue between Ikem Osodi and the policeman is significant:

>»So when you see electric for somebody's wall it follow say you no go put your parking light? What section of Traffic Law be that one?« »It's a matter of commonsense, I should say.« »Commonsense: So me self I no get commonsense: na so you talk. Ok, Mr. Commonsense, make I see your particulars.«

The ignorance of this policeman and his predilection for making his presence obnoxious indicates that the problem of power wielders is embedded in the social structures. This incident also shows that there

is a particularly harmful way in which the hope of improving the
performance of power by changing its personnel prevents us from
getting to grip with the root of the problem,[7]

for the change from a civilian to a military government
masks the basic flaw in the society which is lack of wisdom in the
use of power. The ordinary soldiers and policemen, who should
have an affinity with the poor downtrodden people, rather exhibit
degenerate vices. Incidents of corruption, like the extortion of
money from commercial vehicle drivers, and even rape, are
associated with them. The author states that "teasing the Kangan
Mobile Police is worse than challenging a hungry Alsatian"
(p.173), and Chris Oriko, on the run from security men, is killed
because he tries to prevent a policeman from raping a girl. The
excesses of His Excellency are thus adopted by ordinary
policemen and soldiers including his favourite expression,
"Kabisa". These pervasive acts of destruction are used by the
author to make forceful the idea that power could be wielded by
any member of the society towards negative purposes.

The tragedy of *Anthills of the Savannah* is felt through
Elewa, the girlfriend of Ikem Osodi, and Beatrice, the girlfriend
of Chris Oriko, who, as the centre of consciousness in the novel,
gathers the broken human fragments together in her home. The
remark which Beatrice makes to Captain Abdul Medani and
Emmanuel, the intelligent student leader, lies at the heart of the
novel. She asks: "what must a people do to appease an embittered
history?" (p.220). Part of the answer to this question is her
comment that "this world belongs to the people of the world not
to any little caucus, no matter how talented" (p.232). This
injunction makes it noteworthy that Achebe, through the
metaphor of power, is saying that a country is not owned by the
few privileged individuals who fritter away the resources of the
society in repetitive unproductive internal battles for social,
economic and political power.

Achebe also shows through the use of irony, symbols and
imagery in the narrative structure of *Anthills of the Savannah* an

---

7    Andrew Czartoryski: *Education for Power.* (London, 1975), p. 19.

34

unpleasant portrait of a society pressurized by social forces that are pushing it to a brink of disaster. However, the novel ends on an optimistic note through the unification of the forces represented by Elewa, Beatrice, Braimoh, Medani and Emmanuel, which gives an indication of the visionary direction to which their potentials could lead the society. It is equally significant that these characters represent varied important occupations in society that include a taxi driver, a student, a sales girl, a soldier and a senior government official. Moreover, this motley but powerful crowd is controlled by the woman Beatrice who justifies the assertion that those

> ...who have thus far felt the lack of an important female character in Achebe's works will be pleased with this latest novel. In many ways, complex and intelligent Beatrice Okoh, the pivotal figure in Anthills is Achebe's most complex portrait of a woman.[8]

However, the novel proceeds beyond this positive depiction of womanhood to cast insight on human frailties and its effects on society. The individual experiences, strengths and frailties of the characters are carefully magnified to reveal the complexity of the wider society where power materializes through deliberate actions and unforseen incidents to affect events and people. Achebe therefore creatively illustrates much of the contemporary tribulations of the African socio-political reality through a metaphoric depiction of power in human interactions.

This article was presented as a paper at the 14th International Conference of the African Literature Association of America, Dakar, March 1989.

---

8   Fiona McLaughlin: "Reading Achebe: A Review of *Anthills of the Savannah.*" *The Gar* 35 (April 1988), p. 22.

Omar Sougou

# LANGUAGE, FOREGROUNDING AND INTERTEXTUALITY IN *ANTHILLS OF THE SAVANNAH*

In *Anthills of the Savannah*,[1] Achebe remains faithful to the didactism which he conceives of as being the onus of the writer whose mission precludes non-commitment. He himself metaphorically derides lack of commitment in these verse lines:

> ... I'm
> told the owl too wears wisdom
> in a ring of defence round
> each vulnerable eye securing it fast
> against the darts of sight.[2]

Unlike the owl, the sexagenarian author of *Anthills of the Savannah* does not seem to wear wisdom like a mask to fence his sight off from the political and social developments in the African continent. In this novel he is likely to be implementing another proverb which is recurrent in *Arrow of God*: "When an adult is in the house the she-goat is not left to suffer the pains of parturition on its tether" (p.21). *Anthills of the Savannah* peruses and probes into the world of power and military dictatorship. It seems to be a sequel of *A Man of the People* which ended with a military takeover, and thus turned out to be prophetic in real life.

---

1 *Anthills of the Savannah*. (London: Heinemann, 1987) appears in this article as *Anthills*. References to Achebe's other novels are to the African Writers Series: *Things Fall Apart* (1958), *No Longer At Ease* (1960), *Arrow of God* (1964) and *A Man of the People* (1966).

2 "NON-commitment". *Christmas in Biafra and Other Poems*. (New York, 1973), pp. 48-49. Achebe wrote about commitment in essays like "Africa and her Writers" and "The Novelist as Teacher" collected in *Morning Yet on Creation Day* (London, 1975). See also *Hopes and Impediments* (London, 1988). Achebe speaks about art and commitment, poetics, society and Igbo philosophy in an interview given in 1985: "An Interview with Chinua Achebe", by J.O.J Nwachukwu-Agbada, *Massachussetts Review*, 28.2 (1987), pp. 273-285.

This fictional work set in the imaginary state of Kangan could apply to many African countries. His Excellency, the General, called Sam by his friends, rules despotically surrounded by a cowering and mostly unscrupulous cabinet. The novelist exposes power politics, opportunism and cynicism in the metonymic state of Kangan. Nuruddin Farah rightly describes *Anthills* as a "most charming novel, a book of metonyms, a rich treasure of transferred meanings."[3] The latter quality makes it textually engaging. It resides in its elaborate underlying semiotic codes that are sustained by the marked self-consciousness at work in it. *Anthills* is similar to the "story" which the elderly leader of the Abazon delegation says, is "like fire, when it is not blazing it is smouldering under its own ashes or sleeping and resting inside its flint-house" (p.124).

Accordingly, anyone discussing it may only tell "little scraps of tale bubbling in [him or her]". Thus, what such a person comes up with might just be "like the middle of a mighty boa which a foolish forester mistakes for a tree trunk and settles upon to take his snuff" (p.125). However great the risks of sharing the forester's ridicule, this work is so exciting that it is worth venturing into it.

In *Anthills* the reader encounters a singular fictional practice in comparison to the former novels. While each of those came with fresh stylistic elements of their own, this one sets out to defamiliarize the reader with the generally conventional narrative discourse that has been used so far. The texture of *Anthills* combines traits met in the earlier novels such as those pertaining to the narrative voice, the ordering of events, and the handling of language. Moreover, it incorporates a number of sub-texts deriving from Achebe's earlier fiction, poetry, essays, and literary criticism. All of these are compounded with textual borrowings from, and reference or allusion to other writers. The artefact results in an intertext and makes *Anthills* appear foregrounded in connection with the preceding novels. On the thematic level, the treatment of a female character, Beatrice, and the approach to the question of woman through her, both function

---

3   "A Tale of Tyranny". *West Africa*, 21 September 1987, pp. 1828-1831.

as significant developments; hence, they are part of the foregrounding scheme. In this paper I propose to study the form of the narrative discourse first. Secondly, I shall investigate how the use of language and intertextuality serves the writer's aim. Thirdly, and finally I offer an analysis of Achebe's reappraisal of women's role, centred on Beatrice.

*Anthills* is based on specular structures in that the narrative is focalized through each of the three main characters in turn: Christopher Oriko (Chris), the Commissioner for Information; Ikem Osodi, the editor of the National Gazette and Beatrice Okoh, Senior Assistant Secretary in the Ministry of Finance. Each of them is a reflector through whom we learn about the others and about His Excellency, the General and head of the state, Sam. The first three characters take turns to tell the story while an omniscient narrator - a narrator in the first degree - supersedes them very often.[4]

The reader of Achebe's earlier novels notices here a significant disruption in the narrative format in terms of the ordering of events and the number of voices intervening in the narration. At first one gains the impression that the story is going to be told entirely by Chris as he starts doing so in the first chapter, "First Witness-Christopher Oriko", this in the manner of Odili, the hero-narrator of *A Man of the People*. But soon after the first chapter Chris is stripped of his testimonial role to be substituted by an extradiegetic/heterodiegetic narrative medium, i.e. a "third person" omniscient narrator who operates outside the story. This same narrator leads us to the third chapter, introduces Ikem and sets the background of the tussle between Chris and him. Thus, Chris becomes a narrator in the second degree and this new voice steps in as a narrator in the first degree. As a result, one is induced to assume that the story will be channelled in duplex, that is, through the interplay of these two voices, only

---

4    I borrowed the term "narrator in the first degree" from Gerard Genette's *Narrative Discourse*, transl. Jane E. Lewin (Ithaca, NY, 1980). I employ here a few items of his terminology like "focalization", "narratee", and the terms describing the status of the narrator that are derived from diegesis.

to discover a new twist in chapter four. All of a sudden the first person pronoun "I" appears, and connects the narrator's voice to Ikem Osodi who is termed "Second Witness" in the chapter heading. We are back to the testimonial function Chris was given in the opening section.

It looks as though the absence of the omniscient narrator in the first chapter and his withdrawal in the fourth, where he allows Chris and Ikem to communicate directly to the narratee as "witnesses", were ploys for the narrator in the first degree to sustain an illusion of objective perspective. In conferring the narrative point of view on these characters involved in the management of State affairs, he seems both to distance himself from the government circle, and to admit to the limits of his omniscience. Thus, he poses as someone who is not allowed access to the arcane of the ruling elite. Then, how can we explain his presence in His Excellency's office in the second chapter? A concern for verisimilitude may account for this since Chris is not endowed with ubiquitousness: he cannot remain in the meeting room while his mind's eye follows His Excellency when he withdraws to consult with Professor Okong, the Commissioner for Home Affairs. In the end, this narrator's game, as it were, turns inconclusive and perhaps self-deceptive for he becomes the all-knowing and omnipresent witness.

This narrator now assumes a first degree status and pursues his regulated apparitions and withdrawals right through Chapter Six, which is entitled "Beatrice". One should note that she is not called forth as a witness like Chris and Ikem even though she intervenes in the narrative in the same way as they do by telling the story in the first person singular in chapters Six and Seven. She functions more like a judge than a witness in the course of the story. She becomes a pivot around whom the narrative revolves in that she is in touch with all the other protagonists.

In Chapter Six Beatrice recounts the episode at the President's private reception. As a reflector, she registers the interests of the members of the coterie who surround His Excellency (Sam), "the new power-brokers" (p.76). These are chiefly Miss Lou Cranford, an American journalist suspected of being a CIA agent, a local tycoon, the Director of the State

Research Council - a euphemism for the secret police - and the Chief of Army Staff, General Ahmed Lango. Interestingly, she writes a pseudo-autobiography within the novel.

Even more interesting is that a new leap occurs in Chapter Eight, "Daughters", which is split into two suggestive sub-headings: "Idemili" and "Nwanyibuife." It comes in the form of a syntactic pointer, "we," the second word of the opening sentence, which indicates that the other voice which has been hitherto outside the narrative is drawing itself into it, becoming that of a homodiegetic narrator. Thereupon any distancing himself from the story, events, and characters is subverted. This voice does not sound like a choral one, signalling a communal narrator. Neither is it indicative of the presence of a raconteur and participant in the story (a homodiegetic/intradiegetic narrator). It rather sounds like a generic, impersonal reference.

However, a closer examination reveals a narrator who consciously appears and speaks to the reader. Taking over Beatrice's autobiography, he tells us: "She was born as we have seen into a world apart." Further on he says: "Barely, we say though, because she did carry a vague sense more acute at certain critical moments than others of being two different people" (p.105). These utterances are clear indicators of a narrator who makes his presence felt, and is very close to Beatrice. In fact, he gradually merges his voice with hers afterwards. This is apparent in the rendering of Beatrice's thought process in page 109. At a first stage, namely in the second paragraph, her internal speech is reported in the direct speech mode:

> These birds, she thought, did not just arrive here this morning.
> Here, quite clearly, is where they have always slept. Why have I
> not noticed them before? (p.109) [Emphasis mine]

Then the following paragraph is reported in the third person by the narrator in the first degree, who in the next paragraph, leaves the floor. Subsequently, all is focalized through Beatrice by way of free-direct speech as can be seen here:

> Beatrice smiled wryly. So, two whole generations before the likes
> of me could take a first class degree in English, there were
> already barely literate carpenters and artisans of British rule
> hacking away in the archetypal jungle and subverting the very
> sounds and legends of daybreak to make straight my way.
> (p.109) [Emphasis mine]

This fusing of the voices of the narrator in the first degree and Beatrice's well after she has officiated as narrator makes her the centrepoint of the novel. From that moment and onwards almost everything is channelled through, or at least, associated with her. In this connection, her being introduced as the last of the three homodiegetic/intradiegetic narrators may be part of a scheme to put her in a central position, because, henceforth, she secures the role of central consciousness, and takes priority over Ikem who can also claim such a status. Besides, she survives both her co-narrators: Chris and Ikem.

The conglomeration of points of view through which the story is mediated results in the partition of the narrative into variegated segments arranged in an unconventional chronological order. One example may suffice to illustrate the point: the account of a single day's events - Ikem's driving to the palace and his meeting with the Abazon delegation at their hotel, starts in Chapter Three then stops, to be resumed in Chapter Nine. The spatial gap is filled with insights into the characters of Ikem, Beatrice and Chris, and the party at John Kent's (alias Mad Medico) in Chapter Five which Chris narrates. This function is an occasion for eliciting more information about His Excellency's past.

On the whole, in this one novel Achebe subsumes narrative techniques he has individually implemented in each of his four prior novels. In *Things Fall Apart* and *Arrow of God* he employs homodiegetic-heterodiegetic narrators who recount events in the manner of the traditional story-tellers. These narrators sound like the West African griot. Consider for example the beginning of *Things Fall Apart*:

> Okonkwo was well-known throughout the nine villages and even
> beyond. His fame rested on solid personal achievements. As a

young man of eighteen he has brought honour to his village by
throwing Amalinze the Cat. (p.3)

In *Arrow of God* the same voice reports the events assuming
the same perspective save, perhaps, the audible comment in the
two final pages of the novel:

Perhaps, it was the constant, futile throbbing of these thoughts
that finally left a crack in Ezeulu's mind. Or perhaps his
implacable assailant having stood over him for a little while
stepped on him as on an insect and crushed him under the heel in
the dust. [...] If this was so then Ulu had chosen a dangerous
time to uphold this wisdom. [Emphasis mine] (pp. 229-230)

The part of speech "perhaps", iterated in the second
sentence and the concessive clause in the third disclose a narrator
involving himself in the matters he relates, thus obliterating any
distance. The narrator of *No Longer at Ease* does likewise by
concluding the story in this way: "And we must presume that, in
spite of his certitude, Mr Green did not know either." (p.154)
[Emphasis mine]

By contrast, one meets a homodiegetic-intradiegetic
narrator, Odili, in *A Man of the People*. This protagonist alone
narrates the events throughout the novel. He begins the story with
these words:

No one can deny that Chief the Honourable M. A. Nanga, M.P.,
was the most approachable politician in the country. [...] I have
to admit this from the outset or else the story I'm going to tell
will make no sense. (p.1)

This device consisting in having the story told by Odili, the
hero, puts a consistent distance between the author and it.[5] In
view of this, distance regulation appears utterly uneven as regards
*Anthills*. The voice-shifting and the dovetailing together of
narrative blocks would finally buttress the self-conscious style of

---

5  Gareth Griffiths: "Language and Action in the Novels of Chinua Achebe",
*African Literature Today*, 5 (1971), 88-105.

the novel. At one point the author, like a conjurer who reveals his magic tricks, emphatically indicates:

> ... and in the background the narrator's voice coming through and declaiming: It is now up to you women to tell us what has to be done. And Agatha is surely one of you. (p.184).

Following this, the narrating voice utters questions such as "And do you know what?" and "How about that?" (pp.184-185). At this juncture it is useful to note that this stylistic pun and the discursive segment wedged between these two phrases are remarks about the women in the story. Moreover, the device points to a fusion of the author's voice and that of the narrator in the first degree to whom the former refers, which results in a distinguishable authorial tone.

As a writer truly aware of the power of language, Achebe impressively monitors it here.[6] The pervasive use of Pidgin as idiolect for character identification as with the half-literate Elewa and the taxi-drivers, or its occurrence in informal speech, or else for phatic purposes as when Beatrice speaks to Elewa, are illustrative of the author's concern for linguistic mimetism.[7] Besides, he achieves sound satirical and other implicit effects by dextrous manipulation of language.

The dramatic utterance which opens the novel - especially: "Finish, Kabisa! Any other business?"- portends the serious happenings in the unfolding of the story. Furthermore, the blunt, dismissive and authoritarian tone is suggestive of the tyrannical rule of His Excellency the General. The sterile language of the General coupled with the semantic misuse of the word "flaunt" by the Attorney-General, which Chris rectifies as "flout" (p.5),

---

6   See "Language and the Destiny of Man" and "The African Writer and the English Language" in *Morning Yet on Creation Day*, op.cit.

7   "Chinua Achebe: Interview", with Anna Rutherford, *Kunapipi*, 9.2 (1987),pp. 1-7. Tony Obilade discusses the use of Pidgin in "The Stylistic Function of Pidgin English in African Literature: Achebe and Soyinka". *Research in African Literatures*, 9 (1978), pp. 433-443. See also Norman Page: *Speech in the English Novel* (London, 1988), pp. 83-84.

connote a linguistic deficiency which is indicative of the cabinet's mediocrity, and correlate with the dearth and harshness that run through *Anthills of the Savannah.*

By contrast, the language of the head of the Abazon delegation reunites the reader with traditional rhetoric based on proverbs as in *Things Fall Apart* and *Arrow of God.*[8] The narrator underscores "the compelling power and magic" in the voice of the elderly leader (p.122). Achebe conveys a highly figurative speech through this nameless white-bearded Abazon deputy. The solemnity of the moment is such that the writer graphologically marks the narrator's voice with italics so as to emphasize the speaker's. One can posit that the author craftily uses the elder's speech as a vehicle for his ideas relating to his position as a writer in the face of the political and social issues. In this, the novel can be viewed as what Roland Barthes calls a "writerly text," that is, a text which offers the reader the opportunity to gain access to the signifier and to the pleasure of writing.[9]

Achebe's posture can be decoded within the network of proverbs and ideophones. A bold reading of Chapter Nine, "Views of Struggle," may equate the parabolic implication in the fable of the tortoise and the leopard with the author's own statement. When the leopard told the tortoise he had caught at last, to prepare to die, the quarry asked for a few moments to prepare his mind for his fate, and started to scratch the road with his hands and feet. In doing this the tortoise wanted to leave traces of struggle that would testify to his resistance. Achebe seems to be saying through the old man's parable that like the

---

8   For a fuller study of proverbs in the works of Achebe refer to Bernth Lindfors: "The Palm Oil with which Achebe's Words Are Eaten". *African Literature Today*, 1 (1968), pp. 3-18; and Chukwuma Okoye: "Achebe: The Literary Function of Proverbs and Proverbial Sayings in Two Novels". *Lores and Language*, 2.10 (1979), pp. 45-63, (Centre for English Cultural Tradition and Language, University of Sheffield).

9   *S/Z*, trans. Richard Miller (London, 1975), p.4; Ben Stoltzfus expands on this point saying: "Writerly works, because they depend so much on "the play" of language, seem by their very nature to generate multiple meanings": Alain Robbe-Grillet: *The Body of the Text* (London, Toronto, 1985), pp.128-129.

tortoise he would have left the marks of his kind of struggle. Thus, the elder's last words become meaningful:

> My people, that is all we are doing now. Struggling. Perhaps to
> no purpose except that those who come after us will be able to
> say: True, our fathers were defeated but they tried. (p.128)

Significantly, Ikem Osodi, who is very likely Achebe's alter-ego, hammers the point home in his lecture at the University of Bassa, this time in a new speech mode, an alloy of traditional imagery and modern phraseology. It is worth noting that Ikem is inspired by the metaphoric discourse of the elder of Abazon, whose story he uses as preamble to his talk. It is not so much the lecture, only the gist of which we are given, that is important as the extensively narrated ensuing debate. Ikem's replies combine to read like an essay on the theme of writers and politics. In humorous but genuinely serious statements Ikem expounds the moral in the fable the author of which, the elder of Abazon, is held in solitary confinement at the Bassa Maximum Security Prison: Because storytellers are a threat:

> They threaten all champions of control, they frighten usurpers of
> the right-to-freedom of the human spirit - in state, in church or
> mosque, in party congress, in the university or wherever.(p.153)

In the lecture Ikem takes to task ideologues, leftist academics, the Bassa Rotary Club and the concept of aid to the Third World. The keynote, however, is the role of the writer. The following lines ring like the author's defensive argument:

> The charge of elitism never fails to amaze me because the same
> people who make it will also criticize you for not prescribing
> their brand of revolution to the masses. A writer wants to ask
> questions. These damn fellows want him to give answers. [...]
> »Give us a miracle! Give us a miracle and we will believe in you.
> Cut out the parables and get to the point. Time is short! We want
> results! Now, now!« [...] As a writer I aspire only to widen the
> scope of that self-examination. I don't want to foreclose it with a
> catchy, half-baked orthodoxy. My critics say: there is no time for
> your beautiful educational programme; the masses are ready and

will be enlightened in the course of the struggle. And they quote Fanon on the sin of betraying the revolution. They do not realize that revolutions are betrayed just as much by stupidity, incompetence, impatience and precipitate action as by doing nothing at all. (pp.157-158)

There is no ambiguity in this type of speech. Then follows in the same tone a diatribe against a kind of radicalism consisting in blaming the ills that affect the nation exclusively on capitalism and imperialism while overlooking the phenomena they engender: bribery, embezzlement and fraud, which should also be extirpated. Ikem concludes his talk aphoristically: "Writers don't give prescriptions, [...] "They give headaches!" (p.161). In this episode the author inserts a real essay, a sub-text, in the intertextual fabric of the narrative by means of his parody of a university lecture. This turns out to be an efficient way to convey his satire of intellectual debates.

Achebe's allegorical language in this book owes much to intertextuality. The intertextual construct of *Anthills* rests on a number of allusions, parodies and direct references to Achebe's own work and to that of other writers which are ingrained in the main text. Michael Riffaterre calls these pre-existing word groups "hypograms" in his study of poetry, but this term can usefully be applied in a discussion of intertextuality in fiction.[10] In the intertext which *Anthills* is, these hypograms are sometimes overt, sometimes covert. They can also be either elevated or just trivial, but in either case they are not innocent.

One example of trivial intertextuality which reveals itself as important is the "green bottles," a hypogram generated by a nursery rhyme. Achebe's intertext transfers the denotative, simple value of the rhyme to a highly connotative level. He makes of the three green bottles a metaphoric representation of the precarious situations of Chris, Ikem, and Sam - the trinity who thought they

---

10 *Semiotics of Poetry*. (Bloomington, 1978). Of note is Julia Kristeva's seminal work on intertextuality as in *Semiotike* (Paris, 1969) and *La Révolution du langage poétique* (Paris, 1974). Jonathan Culler offers an interesting discussion of Riffaterre's approach to intertextuality in *The Pursuit of Signs: Semiotics, Literature, Deconstruction* (London, 1981).

owned Kangan in the eyes of Beatrice. His Excellency, Sam, and the top-ranking duet (Chris and Ikem) are going to a fall one by one like the bottles hanging on a wall in the nursery rhyme.

Ikem is arrested and killed by Sam's secret police, Chris runs for his life thinking:

> Three green bottles. One has accidentally fallen; one is tilting.
> Going, going, bang! Then we becomes I, becomes imperial We.
> (p.191)

Chris is absurdly shot dead, at point-blank range. Sam, the "I" which becomes "imperial We" is reported missing following a coup. Furthermore, the rhyme turns into a plot ingredient as when Chris, at the time of dying, murmured what sounded like "The Last Grin" (p.216). This phrase proves later to have been misheard, and is decoded in the last pages of the novel by Beatrice:

> What he was trying to say was "The Last Green". It was a private
> joke of ours. The last green bottle. It was a terrible, bitter joke.
> (p.231)

In this manner, the nursery rhyme is made a parable of the precariousness and hazards of power, a major theme in *Anthills*.

The excerpt from David Diop's poem, "Africa," employed as epigraph to Chapter Ten which owes its title "Impetuous Son" to the same work, exemplifies overt intertextuality, where the generative text and the hypogram are acknowledged. The poem in the intertext refers both to Ikem and Africa as the tenors of the metaphor in it which bears on the present circumstances. This is substantiated by the resumption of the reference to the poem in Ikem's meditation prompted by his meeting with the taxi-drivers:

> Therefore what is at issue in all this may not be systems after all
> but a basic human failing that may only be alleviated by a good
> spread of general political experience, slow of growth and
> obstinately patient like the young tree planted by David Diop on
> the edge of the primeval desert just before the year of wonders in

which Africa broke out so spectacularly in a rash of independent nation states! (p.139)

Achebe previously used Diop's metaphor in an essay, "The Writer and his Community", which is of relevance to the matters in *Anthills*. He concludes this essay:

> We can see in the horizon the beginnings of a new relationship between artist and community which will not flourish like the mango-trick in the twinkling of an eye but will rather, in the hard and bitter manner of David Diop's young tree, grow patiently and obstinately to the ultimate victory of liberty and fruition.[11]

"Hymn to the Sun", the epic poem that Ikem composes in Chapter Three constitutes perhaps the most arresting element of intertextuality. It sounds like a compact dirge that epitomizes the predicament of the symbolic, forlorn and drought-stricken province of Abazon. This constituency which refused to vote for his Excellency's life-presidency is branded rebellious. By way of consequence, the régime retaliates by denying it assistance. The work for their bore-holes was stopped. As a result, after two years of suffering Abazon sends a deputation to the Big Chief to say, in the words of their leader:

> ... our own yes and perhaps the work on our bore-holes will start again and we will not all perish from the anger of the sun. We did not know before but we know now that yes does not cause trouble. (p.127).

This event is the bedrock of the story. On the one hand, the visit of the Abazon delegates precipitates the crisis in the novel, on the other, Abazon motivates Ikem's poem. "Hymn to the Sun" is the sub-text within which *Anthills of the Savannah* holds en abyme its own symbol, to paraphrase Roland Barthes.[12] This

---

11 *Hopes and Impediments*, pp. 32-41.
12 Barthes in his foreword to *Les Romans de Robbe-Grillet*, by Bruce Morrissette (Paris, 1963), p. 15. Mise en abyme can be defined as a process of textual instability that results from self-conscious writing and aims at producing impact. So structures en abîme are an aspect of foregrounding.

symbol is the iterative image of dearth fossilized in the title of the novel as well as in these lines of the poem:

> The trees had become hydra-headed bronze statues so ancient that only blunt residual features remained on their faces, like anthills surviving to tell the new grass of the savannah about last year's brush fires. (p.31)

The other noteworthy component of the intertextual construct occurs in the first part of Chapter Eight: "Idemili". It is kindred in tone and content with "hymn to the Sun". The bond is found further into the narrative in the form of a prefix to the initial title of the same poem: "Pillars of Fire". The piece of poetry which Chris reads on the way to Abazon is entitled "Pillars of Fire: A hymn to the Sun" (pp.209-210). The figure "Pillar of Fire" connects by antonymy with that of "Pillar of Water" existent in the legend of Idemili, a hypogram yoked with the narrative. The goddess Idemili was sent by her father the Almighty to bridle Power that was rampaging through the world. Idemili descended from the sky to the earth in the "resplendent Pillar of Water":

> It rises majestically from the bowl of the dark lake pushing itself upward and erect like the bole of the father of iroko trees its head commanding not the forest below but the very firmament of heaven. (p.102)

The legend suggests that man's acquisitiveness and individualistic pursuit transformed the Pillar of Water into "numberless shrine-houses across the country, a dry stick rising from the bare, earth floor."(p.103) The image of the dry stick evokes that of the calcinated trees standing like anthills in Ikem's poem, they are both metonyms of the scourge afflicting Africa in many respects. In the figurative language of the legend and of the novel there is a hint that lust for power and greed curbs creativity. The "Pillar of Water" resembles a phallic symbol in the manner it stands, the water of the lake is female, both are associated with creativity.

The myth of Idemili is central to the narrative. It serves as the vehicle for the metaphoric discourse of the fiction, the hypogram can be traced in *Arrow of God* and in Achebe's poem "Lament of the Sacred Python." In *Arrow of God* the priest of Idemili explains:

> Idemili means Pillar of Water. As the pillar of this house holds the roof so does Idemili hold up the Raincloud in the sky so that it does not fall down. Idemili belongs to the sky [...] (p.50)

"Lament of the Sacred Python", a version of which was previously heard in *Arrow of God* (pages 277-278), provides a key to the riddle underlying the Idemili section in *Anthills*. The last two stanzas of the lament of the sacred python, totemic symbol and messenger of Idemili, help to grasp part of the meaning of *Anthills*:

> And great father Idemili
> That once upheld from earth foundations
> Clouds banks of sky's endless waters
> Is betrayed in his shrine by empty men
> Suborned with the stranger's tawdry gifts
> And taken trussed up to the altar-shrine turned
> Slaughter house for the gory advent
> Feast of an errant cannibal god
> Tooth-filed to eat his fellows.
>
> And the sky recedes in
> Anger; the orphan snake
> Abandoned weeps in the shadows.[13]

Therefore in *Anthills* Idemili, the deity of water and fertility, chastizes common people because of the acts of sanguinary puppet dictators like Sam. In the cryptic language of the novel only Idemili may rescue the nation. Then it is no accident that Beatrice who is closely associated with the Almighty, incarnates hope for redemption. She has a dual

---

13 *Christmas in Biafra and Other Poems*, pp. 72-73.

personality: beside her corporeal nature stands an ethereal essence of which she has long been unaware. The narrator in the first degree and Ikem alone know of her divine attributes. In fact, the latter prompts her to realize her second nature which she acknowledges when thinking: "I do sometimes feel like Chielo in the novel, the priestess and prophet of the Hills and the Caves" (p.114). Here crops up a hypogram connected with *Things Fall Apart* the novel Beatrice alludes to. Interestingly, Chielo stands as the single woman of stature in that novel, and the only person upon whom the exceptionally self-reliant Okonkwo entirely depends to save the life of his child. In the final analysis, the Idemili/Beatrice trope confirms itself as the vehicle of a metaphor conferring a crucial role on women. This is a landmark in Achebe's fiction, consequently the status of Beatrice becomes the major constituent of foregrounding in this novel; thus it invites a comment.

Achebe's treatment of female characters has been criticized.[14] In *Things Fall Apart* women are cast in the background, and are to be kept under control like children. Okonkwo beats his wife. A faint-hearted male person is likened to a woman. Yet, there is a redemptive aspect of womanhood which is limited to the woman's protective and nurturing function. This novel popularized the phrase "mother is supreme". It assumes significance when Okonkwo is banished from his village for being guilty of manslaughter. He then seeks refuge in his motherland. In *Arrow of God* women keep a low profile, Ezeulu the priest and the other men monopolize the scene.

In the novels set in the few years before and after independence, women remain confined in secondary roles. *No*

---

14 Carole Boyce Davies: "Motherhood in the Works of Male and Female Igbo Writers". *Ngambika: Studies of Women in African literature*, eds. Carole Boyce Davies/Anne Adams Graves (Trenton, NJ, 1986), pp. 241-256. Kirsten Holst Petersen: "First Things First: Problems of a Feminist Approach to African Literature", *Kunapipi*, 6.3 (1984), pp. 35-47. Merun Nasser: "Achebe and His Women: A Social Science Perspective", *Africa Today* 27.3 (1980), pp. 21-28.

*Longer at Ease* presents Clara as a victim unable to cope with the situation in which she finds herself. The novelist seems to let her sink. In *A Man of the People* there is a host of women, but they generally serve the sexual or political ends of Chief Nanga, with the exception of Eunice.

Eunice is a lawyer, a graduate of the London School of Economics like her fiancé, Max, the leader of the new radical party opposed to Chief Nanga. She is shown as a confident, intelligent woman who intimidates a man like Odili, the narrator. However, she seldom appears in the story, and when this does happen, she sits back while Max is in charge. It is when the latter is assassinated that she acts, shooting the political figure whose thugs committed the murder. In the way he handles Eunice, Achebe fails to project the image the reader is led to expect when she appears for the first time in the novel. It looks as though she is reduced to the stereotyped image of the supporting woman.

*Anthills of the Savannah* ushers in Beatrice as a central figure. To this forename her parents added another one fraught with significance: "Nwanyibuife - a female is also something" (p.87). She could be one of those professional women Kenneth Little wants to see portrayed in African literature.[15] She holds university qualifications and the position of Senior Assistant Secretary at the Ministry of Finance. This is how she presents her conception of life:

> I was determined from the very beginning to put my career first and, if need be, last. That every woman wants a man to complete her is a piece of male chauvinist bullshit I had completely rejected before I knew there was anything like Women's Lib. You often hear our people say: But that's something you picked up in England. Absolute rubbish! There was enough male chauvinism in my father's house to last me seven reincarnations! (p.88)

15 *The Sociology of Urban African Women's Image in African Literature* (London, 1980), pp. 157-158.

As seen earlier, Achebe deftly promoted Beatrice as the central consciousness by making her the converging point of the main characters. As for Elewa, even though Beatrice overshadows her, she proves articulate and aware of women's predicament. One agrees with Ifi Amadiume who points out that "Elewa's strength and confidence means that Beatrice's class superiority over her does not affect her in any way."[16] What is more, Achebe explicitly recognizes her as the representative of the masses of people.[17]

On the other hand, unlike Eunice, Beatrice is not bound to disappear at the end of the story. She becomes a nucleus around which aggregate the forces Achebe regards as capable of defeating the military dictators. At this stage, she clearly fulfils the role of the goddess-like figure which has been ascribed to her. In a more earthly manner, Beatrice embodies women's will to recover their prerogatives as Achebe suggests again in her initiative to preside over the naming of Elewa's baby, a man's privilege. This gesture together with the birth of the child, a metaphorical motif in fiction usually synonymous with hope for the future, and the cluster of the representatives of the various social strata around her, confirm her leading role in the change that is to come.

There is a striking similarity between the functions of Beatrice and Medina, the heroine of Nurrudin Farah's Sardines. Both of them dissent unremittingly from the compromising attitudes of their male partners towards totalitarian rulers. Similarly, they are unbending to the dictators' demands, and each of them is a rallying point of the dissenting forces. Besides one finds some similarity of views between Farah and Achebe with regard to their concern for human rights in general. But Farah has demonstrated a longer standing interest in women's liberation in his fiction. By creating Beatrice as an outstanding female character, Achebe recasts the view of women apparent in his previous work. "In mapping out in detail what woman's role is

---

16 "Class and Gender in *Anthills of the Savannah*: A Critique", *PAL Platform*, 1.1 (London, March 1989), 8-9.
17 Achebe interviewed by Anna Rutherford, *op.cit.*

going to be, I am aware that radical new thinking is required," he admits when speaking about his latest novel, and adds:

> The quality of compassion and humaneness which the woman brings to the world generally has not been given enough scope up till now to influence the way the world is run. We have created all kinds of myths to support the suppression of the woman, and what the group around Beatrice is saying is that the time has now come to put an end to that. I'm saying the woman herself will be in the forefront in designing what her new role is going to be, with the humble co-operation of men.[18]

As far back as 1976 he admitted to being confused about women's role in modern society; he was "not very clear on just how to handle the subject".[19] This is more likely to explain why women in the earlier novels, especially Clara in *No Longer at Ease* and Eunice in *A Man of the People*, were not given full scope to bloom than Achebe's more recent comment that those novels "were also descriptive of the role of women frozen in time".[20] The concept of "women frozen in time" is tenable only in fictional perspective, in real life people are part of the dynamics of history. Hence they cannot be static, then the roles of people like Clara and Eunice involved in the changing times of the fifties into the early sixties should not have been seen as frozen, all the more so as Achebe's fiction is mostly mimetic. Where Beatrice might have been considered an acceptable portraiture of a modern African female character, Amadiume finds shortcomings in Achebe's attempt to delineate her as a strong independent career woman. She takes issue with the fact that Beatrice does not measure up to a fully liberated woman. Arguing that Achebe's paradigm is masculine, and that the story rests on power relations between men, she underscores the lack of relationship between the women who do not even bother to discuss their men. Moreover, and very relevantly to the foregoing

---

18 *Ibid.*, p.4.
19 Victoria K. Evalds: "An Interview with Chinua Achebe". *Studies in Black Literature*, 18.1 (1977), 16-20.
20 Achebe interviewed by Anna Rutherford, *op.cit.*, p.4.

discussion of the Idemili tropology, Amadiume disagrees with Achebe's handling of the concept of divinity which reflects male bias in that God becomes a man and a father to Idemili. Amadiume does not know any linguistic evidence in Igbo to justify this. Neither does she find "any cultural prescription for the filial subordination of the "powerful divine goddess Idemili to this he-god". To her knowledge the female deity is usually given a husband, but not a father.[21]

In her critique Amadiume uncovers "many chinks" in the author's armour in the same way as Beatrice, in the novel, points to the "chinks" in Ikem's commitment. Such criticism may be levelled at many male writers and critics. Whatever their endorsement of women's cause may be, they can only approximate to the facts. No one is able to render women's condition and aspirations better than women themselves. While it is undisputed that male writers and critics can only offer vicarious views in relation to the feminist question, they may communicate their solidarity or sympathy to women's struggle in the way they can. It is an achievement of the Women's Liberation movement that male novelists, critics and reviewers now feel the compulsion to rectify their attitudes.[22]

---

21 "Class and Gender in *Anthills of the Savannah*: A Critique". For an extensive anthropological and gender-centred study of Idemili see Ifi Amadiume's *Male Daughters Female Husbands: Gender and Sex in an African Society* (London, 1987).

22 This article is a slightly revised version of a paper presented at the ACLALS Silver Jubilee conference at Canterbury, Kent, in August 1989.

*Chimalum Nwankwo*

# SOOTHING ANCIENT BRUISES:
# POWER AND THE NEW AFRICAN WOMAN
# IN CHINUA ACHEBE'S
# *ANTHILLS OF THE SAVANNAH*

In a recent interview in connection with his new novel, Achebe said that:

> ... the members of my generation are living, you might say at the cross-roads of different eras. This is a very powerful place in African mythology. The cross-roads is where things meet: where spirits meet human beings, where water meets land, where the sky meets the horizon.[1]

*Anthills of the Savannah* deconstructs this African mythological confluence and compels all components to stand apart separately for scrutiny. Presumptions are challenged and examined. No matter which way a question is turned, every answer points at the nature of power: Is power being used fairly or unfairly? What social posture or ideology assures fair representation and protection? How should common people relate to those in power? How do women fit into the entire equation? Because the human condition is too complex for an either/or solution, the novel offers for answer a package in which grand positions and issues are either reduced to the commonplace or destroyed entirely.

The key to an understanding of this dynamic process is in the subtext of *Anthills of the Savannnah* which has been aptly described as a "tyranny of clowns".[2] Those controlling power in the novel become clowns when we consider the lofty associations

---

1 Bruce Steele: "Conference looks at dancing masks of African Literature." *Pitt University Times* 20.15 (March 31, 1988), p. 5.
2 Nadine Gordimer: "A Tyranny of Clowns". *New York Times*, February 21, 1988. Review of *Anthills of the Savannah*.

which Achebe evokes to enforce that notion. There is an echo of Christian infallibility in the choice of a trinity to "constitute" the rulership of Kangan, the imaginary African country where the story is set. His Excellency and his boyhood friends Chris Oriko - the information minister - and Ikem Osodi, the poet and editor of the Government Gazette, ought to constitute effective power, but they do not. The arrogance and despotism of His Excellency makes this impossible. Another Christian echo is added when Chris Oriko ruminates "about my colleagues, eleven intelligent men, educated men who let this happen to them ... the cream of our society and the hope of the black race".[3]

This means that the total number of men around this false savior is twelve, a number with the apostolic ring of Christ's disciples. However, His Excellency's twelve is an ineffective twelve, hence their inability to constitute force in any form. The novel is full of religious allusions and echoes with sometimes apocalyptic hints. To an apprehensive Chris Oriko, an equally worried Attorney-General reassuringly says: "Relax, man, relax; the world isn't coming to an end, you know". (p.8) The crowd waiting to see His Excellency is described as a "chanting multitude" (p.8). When His Excellency ends the cabinet meeting, the noise is like that of "a knee-sore congregation rising rowdily from the prayers of a garrulous priest" (p.7). And when Professor Okong is leaving the group to answer His Excellency's summons, he subverts some of the last words of Christ to his disciples: "I go to prepare a place for you gentlemen. But rest assured I will keep the most comfortable cell for myself". (p.9).

Clearly, His Excellency is only comfortable in worshipful surroundings, and nervous otherwise. It does not matter whether the attention is from dubious foreigners with questionable credentials such as the Englishman John Kent, called Mad Medico for his bohemian and prankish ways, or the American girl who totally lacks integrity.

To succeed in the presence of His Excellency means total subservience. This is rewarded either with admission into his

---

3 Chinua Achebe: *Anthills of the Savannah*. (New York: Anchor/Doubleday, 1988), p. 2. Further page references are to this edition.

cabal of executive responsibility with its perquisites or, when ignored, punished with ignominious dismissal, incarceration or death. Dominant, therefore, in the opening of the novel is a slavish humility, especially acute in the buffoonery of Professor Okong. Okong has allowed himself to degenerate from lofty dreams to a bootlicking minister for Home Affairs, from an activist religious minister to a domesticated and amoral politician. It is the Professor who in supreme irony tells His Excellency:

> Your Excellency is not only our leader but also our Teacher [emphasis mine]. We are always ready to learn. We are like children washing only their bellies, as our elders say when they pray. (p.17).

Power may be unassailable from the viewpoint of the wielder but various human actions suggest that the security of power is fragile and illusory. This is the vision which emerges in other different undisguised representations of human action in the novel. In the final analysis, whether in utterance or in action, what the author endorses is caution for whoever dallies with power in any form. There are quite a few examples of that position in the novel. The "traffic conundrum" (p.26) in the "testimony" by Chris Oriko actually spells out the fact that the contest for power is something which the high and low in society have to contend with daily, as mere humans rather than class contestants. In two strong situations in the "testimony" by Ikem Osodi, the conundrum becomes more complex in its defiance of the regular Marxist rubrics of a conscious oppressed, battling the odds erected by organized oppression: In the first instance, as sacred and profane symbols and images jostle for ascendance, one realizes that the task awaiting the activist and the leftist revolutionary is no easy task where the oppressed is clearly ignorant of the fact, the nature or source of oppression.

Here, there is an indication of a social upheaval and the possibility of rebirth. The role of women in the cosmic scheme is expressed as a sub-conscious counter-point in the uneasy silence accompanying the death and last utterance of one armed robber:

> In that brief silence, in a loud and steady voice he proclaimed: "I
> shall be born again!" Twice he said it, or if thrice, the third was
> lost in a new explosion of jeers and lewd jokes and laughter so
> loud that it was clearly in compensation for the terrible truth of
> that silence in which we had stood cowed as though heaven had
> thundered: Be still and know that I am God. The Lady in front of
> me said: "Na goat go born you nex time no to woman". (p.38).

Such dark hints of oppression from a warped consciousness
pervades the novel. The author is carefully insistent about the
resolution of such paradoxes. It is clear from that scene that if
armed robbery is wrong, so also is the method of its punishment.

In a second scene, "a tottering pugnacious drunkard was
provoking a fight with a towering stranger" (p.43). The reaction
of the watching market crowd is in favour of the gentle restraint
of the towering stranger who turns out to be "the new champion
wrestler of Kangan"(p.43). The comparison between such calm
attitudes to power and that of the paranoid bullying of His
Excellency is unmistakable, so also the loyalty of the author.

The subject of power is taken up again in the section,
"Views of Struggle". In the speech by one of the members of the
Abazon delegation, one Igbo proverb reiterates the theme of
effective power, emphasizing its unobtrusive nature in the
introduction of Ikem Osodi: "Our people say that an animal
whose name is famous does not always fill a hunter's basket"
(p.111). Because the rest of the speech unduly dwells on Ikem's
weaknesses, another parabolic statement on art and the conduct of
artists by an older, wiser and more restrained speaker amends the
brash temper of the younger speaker with an extrapolation which
emphasizes the danger, even for artists, in the misuse of power:

> So the arrogant fool who sits astride the story as though it were a
> bowl of foo-foo set before him by his wife understands little
> about the world. The story will roll him into a ball, dip him in
> the soup and swallow him first. (p.114).

Topically, the old man's ire could be directed at those
African writers who imagine that their story telling capability
invests them with infallibility. Such presumed infallibility is by

implication as unconscionable as the self-destructive despotism of the failed African leadership. In all these examples it is implied that tolerance is the consistently missing element in the actions of individuals constituting the polity. It is an impediment to any form of rational organization. This is why all the apparently positive characters in the novel are endorsing a cautious and tolerant attitude in their social relationships. In the section of the novel with the title "Impetuous Son", Ikem Osodi hones up a position which represents in summary fashion an ideological leitmotif of what is beyond any doubt Achebe's position in *Anthills of the Savannah*:

> What is at issue in all this may not be systems after all but a basic human failing that may only be alleviated by a good spread of general political experience, slow of growth and obstinately patient ... (p.128).

Before turning into the issue of women and how Beatrice Okoh fits into the entire picture it is relevant to address the issue of style as a necessary aspect of Achebe's discourse on power. The levels of language in *Anthills of the Savannah* constitute a valid aspect of Achebe's discourse. Power in the novel is monopolistic because of its concentration in one reckless individual. Style in this work counters that monopoly in its eclectic effort to represent the various strata of Kangan society. The sophisticated testimonies of the major witnesses, Chris Oriko, Ikem Osodi and Beatrice Okoh are formal renditions. The vehicle of the less educated in Kangan such as Elewa, the lower echelon of the police force and the people in the streets is pidgin. Ikem's passionate reflections are poetic. The Kangan delegates to Bassa transliterate their regional dialect into an English rich in folklore, proverbs and rural imagery, hallmark of Achebe's earlier *Things Fall Apart* and *Arrow of God*.[4]

This attitude of the author to the various key characters is in keeping with the notion of collective responsibility held by Ngugi

---

4 *Things Fall Apart*. (London: Heinemann, 1958); *Arrow of God*. (London: Heinemann, 1964).

wa Thiong'o in *A Grain of Wheat*.[5] In *Anthills of the Savannah*, Chris Oriko explains why that attitude is the most logical in the light of the social morass: "We are all connected. You cannot tell the story of any of us without implicating the others'"(p.60). Indeed, before His Excellency's death in a coup ends the tragedy, the key characters are effectively neutralized by death, incarceration or psychological battering. The logic of factions and triumphant ideologies is neutralized by Osodi's exchange with students whose unstudied radicalism blinds them of their own flaws. It is ironic and quite significant that Chris Oriko's death is in the hands of one of those whose lot would have improved by Oriko's fight for justice. In the long run, the winning logic is that articulated by Ikem Osodi:

> Those who would see no blot of villainy in the beloved oppressed nor grant the faintest glimmer of humanity to the hated oppressor are partisans, patriots and partyliners. In the grand finale of things, there will be a mansion also for them where they will be received and lodged in comfort by the single-minded demi-gods of their devotion. But it will not be in the complex and paradoxical cavern of mother Idoto. (p.92).

The cavern of mother Idoto, earth spirit, is neither factious nor discriminatory in justice.[6] Even though it is a female spirit, it protects the martial in times of grievances, just as well as it protects the humble at peace time. Foremost therefore, it is all-inclusive. Through Beatrice Okoh, the logic and raison d'etre of this spirit is actualized in *Anthills of the Savannah*. It is through her that the author organizes a methodical subversion of the so-called logos of phallocentrism. Through her, a careful debate neutralizes the oppressive patriarchal logic in a universal psyche in which Africa is as guilty as the West in female oppression.

---

5   Ngugi wa Thiong'o: *A Grain of Wheat*. (London: Heinemann, 1968).
6   Idoto is the goddess in the opening of Labyrinths, the poetry of the late Christopher Okigbo. The crucial aspect of the nature of Idoto is the fact that even though she was a female spirit, supposed to be tender, she was the spirit which accompanied her worshipers to war. Her nature is therefore androgynous in the sense of a balance between male and female energy.

Commenting on Christopher Okigbo's attitude to women in his poetry, Elaine Savony Fido observes that

> the very androgynous quality which often characterizes highly developed creative writers is arguably the result of imaginative effort to transcend gender in order to create a full human canvas...[7]

If androgyny implies a successful neutralization of male or female superiority, Achebe accomplishes the same through reductionist references to the various negative images of women in religious and secular literature. In a debate between Ikem Osodi and Beatrice Okoh, the Old Testament position on women is dismissed as "crude denigration" (p.89). The later New Testament elevation to the pedestal of "the very Mother of God" (p.89) ensures that "she will just be as irrelevant to the practical decisions of running the world as she was in her old days" (p.89). The continuing debate espies "a parallel subterfuge" (p.89) in the African characterization: "Nneka ... Mother is supreme" (p.89). The truth about the human condition actually emerges when in the chapter on "Daughters", the male and female principles in a universalized Igbo cosmos act out a lyrical drama in which Power (man) is redeemed from naked ugliness by woman in much the same acknowledged symbiosis through which Ikem acquires "the gift of insight" (p.88) from Beatrice.

Achebe offers various reasons through parabolic and anecdotal images why Power has been misconstrued by humanity. Here again, his foundry is Igbo creation mythology where Power is like light in its function of nourishment. It is so integral to the world that not even the most delicate efforts to extract the essence of it from its naturale, the reality in the cosmos, has been successful. "Man's best artifice to snare and hold the grandeur of divinity has always crumbled" (p.94).

---

7 Elaine Savory Fido: "Okigbo's Labyrinths and the Concept of Igbo Attitudes to the Female Principle". *Ngambika: Studies of Women in African Literature*, eds. Carole Boyce Davies/Anne Adams Graves. (Trenton, N.J., 1986) p. 227.

Achebe locates the apex of this quest for cosmic inclusiveness in the tragic tale of the Igbo ozo title holder. The Igbo ozo title holder is one who has successfully and humbly accepted the awesome responsibility which power confers on the holder. Significantly, its delicate ritual of moral maturity must be effectuated only with the guidance of a daughter - "a daughter it must be" (p.94) and disobedience is irreverence which attracts certain destruction. A disregard of probity and rectitude also attracts certain destruction. As in the case of the man who, without moral authority, in the name of "randiness" and machismo "performed the rites, took the eagle feather and the titular name Nwakibie" (p.95) retribution and death springs an ambush from the most unlikely of circumstances. Nwakibie means (in Igbo) "the one greater than others". But Nwakibie is tragically brought low by the appearance of the "Daughter of God - the very one who carries not a drop of venom in its mouth and yet is held in greater awe than the deadliest of serpents" (p.96).

On reflection one cannot help dwelling on this image of the "Daughter of God" as it relates to Beatrice, whom Nadine Gordimer characterizes as "one of the most extra-ordinary, attractive and moving women in any contemporary novel".[8] There are comparative efforts in literature and myth where writers engage in the restoration of the female principle, such as in *The White Goddess* by Robert Graves, or the recent works of Ngugi wa Thiong'o.

In comparison, Achebe's art appears to have painted better, into the human canvas, a less obstrusive female image, without erecting a new myth of superiority in the effort to counter the discredited old. Beatrice is distant from the righteous feminist spirits in, for instance, Emecheta's *Double Yoke* or *In the Ditch* hurling stones at masculine arrogance. She is distant from the effective but artificial avenging women of Ngugi's *Petals of Blood* or *Devil on the Cross*. She is not even wholly

> ... like the women in the Sembene film who pick up the spears abandoned by their men folk, for it is not enough that women

---

8   Gordimer, *op. cit.*, p. 1.

should be the court of last resort because the last resort is a damn
sight too far and too late! (p.84).

Beatrice is inextricably part of the human tide. She knows
and accepts, like Chinua Achebe, that "every event has more than
one story."[9] After a childhood rebuff from her mother for taking
sides with her in what she imagines a battering by her father she
learns never to rush to quick conclusions or judgments in life. She
learns to take sides, if ever necessary, slowly and with
circumspection. Beatrice constantly subjects herself to severe
criticism as much as she does every one else or anything
unseemly in society: timid African womanhood, aggressive
feminism, male chauvinism, neo-colonialism. She spares nothing.
Her erotic dance with His Excellency which she sees as "soothing
our ancient bruises together" is an epithet which one may, bar
cavil, apply to the nature of her social commitment. Beatrice is
calm, from her attitude to the stigma of female dependency
through her relationship with her housemaid, the fanatical
Agatha, the poet-intellectual Osodi, the sentient and uneducated
Elewa, and the compassionate and tragic Chris Oriko. She is that
delicate thing which Power strives to be but cannot be; to be
simply respected without being sacralized.
Beatrice is able to be what she is because her Africa, for
women, has changed from an agrarian period in which there was,
even in the farm, merely "women's crops" and then the "king of
crops" for men.[10] In marriage and other sensitive social and
political issues many of the old walls are going down. The
traditional restrictions have been whittled down to such a level
where, as in the novel, even the spirituality which unconsciously
sustains Beatrice is also threatened. The author informs us that, in
the delineation of her duality,

> Beatrice Nwanyibuife did not know these traditions and legends
> of her people which played little part in her upbringing ... but

---

9   Lydia Foerster: "Man of the People", *Daily Texan*, February 19, 1988, p.
    11.
10  *Things Fall Apart*, p. 16.

knowing or not knowing does not save us from being known and
even recruited and put to work" (p.96).

We see in her the workings of an archetype in which
Christian and Igbo myth have united to produce a unique figure, a
prism through which the lineaments of all other major characters
and events are defined. Within the swelling eschatological tide,
the business of salvation is hers as the "Daughter of God", not the
son of God. Accordingly, she states that:

> For weeks and months after I had definitely taken on the
> challenge of bringing together as many broken pieces of this
> tragic history as I could lay my hands on I still could not find a
> way to begin. Anything I tried to put down sounded wrong -
> either too abrupt, too indelicate or too obvious - to my middle
> ear (p.75). [emphasis mine].

In the end, she survives to fight on, attesting through her
general conduct that revolutionary redemption can only be
through the quintessence of delicate action. As Carole Bayce
Davies says,

> While Achebe's works are obvious classics within the African
> literary tradition a re-examination of his work from a feminist
> position reveals woman as peripheral to the larger exploration of
> man's experience.[11]

This position is now obsolete in the light of the revelations
of Achebe's new work. Unless that feminist position elevates
propagandese above classicism, it is very difficult to imagine a
traditional African family situation in which, despite what seems,
the woman is not there in the background as chief broker of
events. One serious flaw in this kind of criticism of African
literature is the tendency to wish away the African reality which
informs some African writers' works.
    There is a clear inability to differentiate the chauvinism
which marginalizes and vitiates female roles from the writers'

---

11 Carole Boyce Davies: "Motherhood in the Works of Male and Female Igbo
   Writers", *Ngambika*, p. 247.

responsibility to retain and reflect that rationally verifiable semblance of reality in any worthwhile fiction. The dominant tissue of Achebe's works is formed by the historification of fictive characters and their total circumstances. Logically then, his earlier artistic creations have been faithful to an Igbo pre-colonial or colonial culture of women in the "minor role" or "the dependency role."[12]

Achebe's attitude to women in *Anthills of the Savannah* is therefore the consequence of present African experience, validating the existence of certain kinds of women enjoying a setting totally different from that of their predecessors. If Beatrice is new, so indeed are her circumstances. Through Beatrice, *Anthills of the Savannah* becomes an update which rests for the author the case of female subservience as moribund historical phenomenon rather than a deliberately contrived chauvinism. Generally, what this new work accomplishes is to emphasize that it is detrimental to foreclose any revolutionary alternative as we grapple with the human condition in Africa. Each strategy of social transformation deserves careful and cautious consideration which above all things recognizes the failings of all human beings as unpredictable trustees of human institutions. Possible political action should therefore be subordinated to a praxis which rejects specific ideological parameters.

What Achebe finally compels the reader to accept is that opposing logic cannot only be contained within one space but can actually offer systemic advantages through complimentarity. The fact that all this chiefly manifests through a woman in a discourse on the nature of power, bolsters this update.

---

12 Esther Y. Smith: "Images of Women in African Literature: Some Examples of Inequality in the Colonial Period.", *Ngambika*, p. 31.

*Tayo Olafioye*

## *MONUMENT TO MADNESS*
## *THE AFRICAN BASILLICA*

*All hail*
*The Ignoble*
*Houphouët Boigny!*
*His Temple of God*
*Our Glorious Poverty*
*At Yamoussoukro*
*This Basillica in the Bush*
*Monument To Infamy*
*Another Taj MarHall*
*At the Altar of our Insanity*
*Where our Emptiness Is mentained.*
*Two Hundred Million Dollars*
*A Land:*
*Two Hundred Million Poverties*
*And God: Already ---*
*Too Many Houses Over-Rich.*
*And Why this largest Costliest*
*in Africa: The Mystery of our Madness*
*History's Home of Histrionics*
*One Man's Monument*
*To Self and Infamy*

*Oh, Africa:*
*Make Not Notoriety our Name*
*This Foolishness My great Sorrow*
*Are We Better Communicants*
*Or Prayers More Sweetly?*
*Every Corner Our pains of Need*
*Even Our Souls*
*Are Termites Disgorged.*

*Patricia Alden*

# NEW WOMEN AND OLD MYTHS: CHINUA ACHEBES'S *ANTHILLS OF THE SAVANNAH* AND NURUDDIN FARAH'S *SARDINES*

One of the triumphs of Beatrice's creation [is that] the things that fell apart under the impact of Europe in Mr. Achebe's first novel...come together in this woman. She is a true world-historical figure in Georg Lukacs's sense, and it is Mr. Achebe's victory that she is also one of the most extraordinary, attractive and moving women characters in any contemporary novel.

(Nadine Gordimer on *Anthills of the Savannah*)

Medina's consciousness, exasperatingly, occupies the largest space in this portrait of embattled Somali womanhood. [In *Sardines*] Farah has warned us...of her egotistical possessiveness towards her daughter and the self-absorbed ideological purity of all her actions. ...Medina's challenges to the regime are merely flamboyant and self-indulgent ideological gestures...The problem is that so much of the narrative is presented from the perspective of this intransigent idealism and coloured by Medina's priggish self-righteousness that these...come to have a ring of doctrinal finality and authorial approval.

(Derek Wright on *Sardines*)

Guided by the above remarks, a reader interested in successful fictional representations of women would with confidence select Achebe's work in preference to Farah's. Achebe's stature as a distinguished novelist is beyond question, and much of *Anthills of the Savannah*[1] is a compelling account of political turmoil in an African nation. However, Achebe's portrait of Beatrice Okoh betrays a significant failure of imagination - a failure to take

---

1 Chinua Achebe: *Anthills of the Savannah*. (New York: Doubleday, 1988). All references are to this edition of the novel, which is abbreviated in this text as *Anthills*.

seriously, as part of contemporary political struggle, the feminist challenge to patriarchal authority, and a corresponding failure to create convincing, interesting women characters. Offered as an example of a new African woman, Beatrice is effectively removed from the brawl of politics to assume traditional roles as her Dantean namesake, as the water goddess Idemili, as Mother Africa. The novel achieves its closure in an uncritically examined connection between the fertility of women and the rebirth of a nation.

It is rather in Nuruddin Farah's novel *Sardines*[2], that we find a genuinely "world-historical" character shaped by the critical contradictions of her time. Moreover, through Medina and her circle of friends Farah captures the diversity in women's experiences. The novel shows their domestic, private lives as being fully imbricated in the political order, and thereby implies how profound the cultural transformation required to free everyone from dictatorship must be. In *Sardines* women's sexuality, a focus of male oppression and female power, associates them not with the fertility goddess Idemili but with Prometheus and the creative and destructive potential of fire. The complexity of his presentation, rich in symbolism, allusion, characterization and multiple points of view, enables Farah to explore important contradictions experienced by Somali women.

Chinua Achebe's *Anthills* and Nuruddin Farah's *Sardines* may be usefully compared in several ways. Both probe the causes for the emergence of dictatorship in post-colonial Africa and both overtly connect feminism to the larger political struggle at the state level. Their female protagonists are ideologically situated in similar ways. Beatrice and Medina belong to an urban elite; both have been well-educated abroad, hold advanced degrees, and are professional women with access to government circles, Medina as a journalist and Beatrice as Senior Assistant Secretary in the Ministry of Finance. Among the privileged of their nation, both feel a responsibility to resist the growing atmosphere of repression. Both women define themselves as feminists who

---

2    Nuruddin Farah: *Sardines*. (London: Heinemann, 1981). All references are to this edition of the novel, which is abbreviated in this text as *Sardines*.

understand that the liberation of women from patriarchy is a necessary part of the social transformation required to bring about a more equitable order. Their intellectual commitment to feminism is sustained in part by their western education, in part by traumatic experiences as children within traditional societies.

For Medina, this includes the experience of vaginal circumcision, for Beatrice, overt disparagement as a daughter and an atmosphere of family violence. Distanced from the majority of women in their countries, Beatrice and Medina each have as a close friend a "woman of the people" in Elewa and Ebla. These friendships allow their ideological commitment to be seen in contrast to a more pragmatic, less theoretical perspective. Medina exists in an extensive network of female relationships, each of which affords the reader a different context in which to assess her. By contrast, Beatrice, though she holds a responsible position in the government, is largely restricted to the role of girlfriend and her author names her as "girl" in contrast to the "men" who are her contemporaries and friends to Elewa.

Husbands, brothers, presidents and politicians figure in *Sardines*, but Farah allows the women characters to fill the foreground in his novel, while Achebe has his few women appearing just over the shoulder of the men on whom he focuses. Farah's larger canvas allows him to represent women's experience as various, with several distinct patterns organizing the text; in Achebe's more sparse world the two women characters become freighted with symbolic significance by way of enriching their presence in the text, and the weight of this symbolic meaning seems to fix and limit them in prescribed roles: woman of the people, goddess and prophetess.

Although, as I shall argue further, Beatrice is diminished in *Anthills* in a variety of ways, it is plausible to compare her with Medina for she is clearly intended to have major standing in the novel, serving with Chris Oriko and Ikem Osodi as one of the narrators of the novel. Her autobiography is at the center of the novel, her past given equal treatment with the men's, and she, like Chris and Idem, is rushing to write down the novel we have before us (*Anthills*, p.75). Thus she lays claim with Chris and Ikem to the important role of story teller, the one who's voice is heard after the battle (*Anthills*, p.113). However, the men are disposed to equate their personal history with "the story of this country" (*Anthills*, p.60) while Beatrice anxiously questions herself: "Who am I that I should inflict my story on the world?" (*Anthills*, p.80). This self-diminishment is troubling, but the real difficulty is that the story she tells about herself is essentially the same as that told by the men. That male and female versions of Kangan history would be the same is itself startling - a failure of the imagination mentioned above - and the more discouraging in a novel which makes it so clear that there are distinct class versions of history, indeed distinct, class-marked languages in which to tell it. While the characters learn they must pay attention to economic divisions, gender differences are represented as resolved, most notably in the projected cross-class marriage of Ikem and Elewa and the uncomplicated, cross-class friendship between Beatrice and Elewa.

Beatrice serves primarily as a guide and teacher of the men. She urges Chris to mend his friendship with Ikem and alerts him to the coming danger from Sam, the President. She educates Ikem, poet and dissident editor of *The National Gazette*, to see the need for including women in new roles in his utopian political order. However, the way in which this education is presented to us is revealing. The scene involves two flashbacks, both narrated by Beatrice. Remembering their university days in London, she says:

> I was determined from the very beginning to put my career first and, if need be, last. That every woman wants a man to complete her is a piece of male chauvinist bullshit I had completely rejected before I knew there was anything like Women's Lib. You often hear our people say: But that's something you picked up in England. Absolute rubbish! There was enough male chauvinism in my father's house to last me seven reincarnations! (*Anthills*, p.80-81)

Beatrice's tone here seems intended to strike us as youthfully shrill. Later she tells Chris that she is, after all, a traditional "girl" who wants a certain kind of "man" to be sexually possessive of her (*Anthills*, p.103). Though we are asked

to take her ideas seriously, her own language works to undermine
the coherence of her feminist position. Despite this dissonance,
Beatrice has an impact on Ikem:

> ... we argued a lot about what I have called the chink in his
> armoury of brilliant and original ideas. I tell him he has no clear
> role for women in his political thinking; and he doesn't seem to
> be able to understand it. (*Anthills*, p.83)

Several years later in Kangan, Ikem appears on Beatrices's
doorstep in the midst of a driving rain, telling her he has come on
a "mission...to thank you for...the gift of insight...into the world
of women" (*Anthills*, p.88). Ikem claims to have learned the folly
of putting women on a pedestal, of being too respectful, of saying
"Mother is supreme" and yet allowing women's participation in
daily affairs only as a last resort. Women, Ikem says, will have to
tell men what "the new role for Woman will be" (*Anthills*, p.90),
characteristically hypostatizing myriad women as "Woman" even
as he speaks of their empowerment. Equally characteristically for
this unreconstructed imagination, Ikem controls all the dialogue
throughout this passage. Though Beatrice is guide, Ikem is the
actor, the speaker, the man in control. She is identified with
Idemili, the goddess who manifests herself "in the resplendent
Pillar of Water" (*Anthills*, p. 93), the environment which enables
male fertility. Not only is Beatrice essentially passive in her role
as goddess/teacher, in the following chapter, which develops her
connection with the goddess; we are told that she is like "the
village priestess" who is ridden by her divinity - that is, the
power possesses her, rather than she possessing the power - and
that, furthermore, Ikem "knew [this] better than Beatrice herself"
(*Anthills*, p.96).
Ikem then abruptly shifts from his impassioned illumination
about women to what we come to feel is the burning issue in this
novel: how to achieve political reform in desperately divided and
underdeveloped societies. This material is couched in
unreconstructed language that refuses to take gender seriously:

> Man will surprise by his capacity for nobility as well as for
> villainy. No system can change that. It is built into the core of

man's free spirit. [...] Experience and intelligence warn us that
man's progress in freedom will be piecemeal, slow and
undramatic. (*Anthills*, p.90)

It may be significant that in this passage, following on the
heels of his effort to acknowledge women as equal partners, Ikem
urges the most cautious kind of reform. "We can only hope to
rearrange some details in the periphery of the human personality.
Any disturbance of its core is an irresponsible invitation to
disaster" (*Anthills*, p.91). Merely expressing the possibility of
women as equal partners prompts the reflection that major
changes will invite disaster. The door is open at this point for
Beatrice to respond to or criticize Ikem, but she is silenced by his
passionate kiss which leaves her "trembling violently...struggling
for air" (*Anthills*, p.92). The storm is over, the goddess Idemili
has manifested herself and given Ikem his insight, and then
moved on.

Beatrice's major action in the novel occurs when she is
invited to the President's for a private dinner; she and Chris
assume she is being asked to advise Sam on the dangerously
widening rift between him and his two oldest friends. But the plot
stalls at this point, and the dinner party becomes trivialized as an
arena for sexual combat. Miffed that she has been invited merely
to provide "the woman's angle" for a visiting white female
American journalist, Beatrice first snubs, then attacks her for her
position on foreign debt. When she sees this "Desdemona" is
seducing the President, Beatrice goes to work to woo him back to
African traditions:

> I did it shamelessly. I cheapened myself. God! I did it to your
> glory like the dancer in a Hindu temple. Like Esther, oh yes like
> Esther for my long-suffering people.
> And was I glad the king was slowly but surely responding! Was I
> glad! The big snake, the royal python of a gigantic erection
> began to stir in the shrubbery of my shrine as we danced closer
> and closer...soothing our ancient bruises....Fully aroused he
> clung desperately to me. (*Anthills*, p.74)

At this point she takes Sam aside to explain that she is merely making a political point. Perhaps not surprisingly, he shows her the door.

In this scene the cheapening of Beatrice and her association with the goddess comports oddly with the seriousness with which both are presented elsewhere. If her feminist consciousness and race-consciousness are meant to be interestingly at odds in this scene, this contradiction is not developed, nor elsewhere alluded to; thus important issues serve as the occasion for a farcical peek at Sam's gigantic erection, at Beatrice's bumps and grinds.

The next chapter opens with Beatrice's autobiography, followed by a lyrical tribute to Idemili, and ending with a scene of love-making between Chris and Beatrice, which we are clearly supposed to take "straight" as she, the goddess, leads him into the depths of her "heaving groves" to "her own peculiar rites over which she held absolute power" (*Anthills*, p.104). Brought to the point of ecstacy, Beatrice now prophesies the climax of the novel:

> I see trouble building up for us. It will get to Ikem first. No joking, Chris. He will be the precursor to make straight the way. But after him it will be you. We are all in it..." (*Anthills*, p.105)

In the coda to the novel, some of the symbolism tries to persuade us further about women's power. With their male lovers dead, Beatrice and Elewa are the nucleus of the new, egalitarian, inclusive community, whose future is promised in the figure of the daughter Elewa bears after Ikem's death. However, this new holy family of women precludes investigation of the ideological differences between Elewa and Beatrice, differences of class which have been at the heart of the novel. Beatrice takes the lead, appropriating a traditionally male role in the naming ritual, giving the daughter a male name, "Amaechina: *May-the-path-never-close.*"

The future she inaugurates appears open to new possibilities, new combinations of male and female roles, new empowerment of ordinary people like Elewa. But Beatrice is upstaged by the arrival of the anarchic figure of Elewa's uncle, drunk and late in arriving for the naming, initially threatening in his peremptoriness, demanding to know who has named the child. When he is told of the non-traditional ceremony, his "explosion into laughter took everybody by surprise and then dragged them all into his bombshell of gaiety." (*Anthills*, p.209). The uncle presides over the breaking of the kola nut, offering a rousing toast which has the effect of fixing our attention on a male speaker who powerfully articulates the vision that has most deeply informed the novel of a humane, inclusive social order in which "all of us" participate. And "all of us" is certainly intended to include the women - women as child-bearers and fertility figures, women as goddesses or Dantean guides to men. But not women as speakers, women as autonomous seekers after their own ends, women who have serious ideological differences to work out, women whose claims to authority must be disruptive. The very sense of unity and resolution here at the end of Achebe's novel testifies to the fact that he has not seriously imagined women as equal participants in making the history of Kangan.

Farah's character Medina is at the center of a novel that is at the center of a trilogy about political oppression in Somalia, a work to which Farah has given the collective title *Variations on a Theme of African Dictatorship*. His representation of women's experience is more impressive than Achebe's, not merely because he affords it more space but because Farah assumes a vital connection between patriarchal and other forms of oppression. In the first volume of the trilogy, *Sweet and Sour Milk*[3], Farah takes as an epigraph to Part II a quotation from Wilhelm Reich:

> In the figure of the father the authoritarian state has its representative in every family, so that the family becomes its most important instrument of power. (Wilhelm Reich)

This quotation is paraphrased by Mursal in *Close Sesame*[4] (p.93-94) and by Sagal in *Sardines* (p.62). The insight is developed throughout the trilogy through conflicts between

---

3   Nuruddin Farah: *Sweet and Sour Milk*. (London: Heinemann, 1979).
4   Nuruddin Farah: *Close Sesame*. (London: Alison & Busby, 1983).

fathers and sons, parents and children, in the rhetoric of the General and the rhetoric of the resistance, in the claustrophobic atmosphere of oppression on the streets and in the homes of the characters. All three novels, but *Sardines* most comprehensively, incorporate the view that patriarchy is a key "variation" of African dictatorship, and indeed the fundamental ground upon which it flourishes.

*Sardines* is about the struggle for control of domestic space and women's bodies, a struggle that affects the lives of all the women in the novel. At the opening, Medina has left her husband Samater, taking their eight-year-old daughter Ubax with her. Her action connects the personal with the political. Samater's mother, Idil, is threatening to circumcise Ubax, a practice which Medina knows personally as a hideous tyranny over women, whether exercized by patriarch or matriarch. Both Medina and Samater belong to the oppositional "Group of Ten", pledged to resist the increasingly terrifying military dictatorship. In the recent past, Medina has been fired, after a four-day stint as editor of the national paper, for challenging the General's censorship. Samater, however, has reluctantly accepted a post in the General's cabinet. She sees him as one who has learned in the bosom of the family to "bow his head" to power and has little confidence that he will resist his mother's mandate for Ubax. Thus she leaves, silently challenging him to resist the dictator at home and in the palace.

Medina's situation is only one variation on the theme of patriarchal control of women's lives. Her mother Fatima has existed in Purdah where she reigns pathetically over children and de facto slaves; her mother-in-law exchanged her body for a bread concession to keep herself and two children from starvation. Amina is raped for her father's complicity with the dictatorship. She resists her father and the General, who are eager to hide this evidence of dissent, by insisting on bearing the child of the rape. A girl of sixteen whose family had emigrated to America is forcibly circumcised on a visit to the coutry to teach her parents a lesson in patriotism. Other stories remind us that even when male power is not direct and brutal, women's bodies provide occasions for control and limitation in patriarchal culture, with its obligatory requirements of virginity and fertility.

Medina's protegee Sagal loses her vaunted autonomy when she finds herself pregnant from a one-night stand, moiling in adolescent confusion. Xaddia is divorced when her husband discovers she uses birth control, Sandra is disfigured by her abortion, and Dulman tormented by her infertility.

These stories represent many ways in which women are trapped in the sardine tin of patriarchal culture. Their responses range from Fatima's passive acceptance to Idil's insistence on her own limited authority, to Ebla's and Dulman's mix of complicity and private refusal, to Medina's determined resistance. By placing Medina within this network of relationships, giving her many roles as mother, daughter, sister, wife, friend, mentor and dissident, Farah allows us to compare her experience with that of other women and to view her from their several perspectives. While her fundamental political understanding is authorially underwritten in the trilogy, the way in which Medina chooses to live is open to criticism and interpretations.

This uncertainty about how we should judge Medina troubles the critic Derek Wright, whose words I quoted at the beginning of this essay. Irritated by her "compulsive [feminist] ideologizing"[5], he finds Medina "egotistically possessive" towards her daughter, given to "flamboyant and self-indulgent" political gestures, and "priggish[ly] self-righteous".[6]

The freedom which Medina forces prematurely upon Ubax is at times almost as oppressive as the obedience Idil has forced upon Samater, her emotional and intellectual tyranny over her daughter as stifling as its physical counterpart...Medina terrorizes her young daughter with knowledge, as does Idil with the circumcisional knife.[7]

Wright's negative, at times belittling assessment of Medina misses the power and appeal, the sheer interestingness of her character. Thus he is puzzled when Medina's closing claim to be

---

5  Derek Wright: "Parents and Power in Nuruddin Farah's *Dictatorship Trilogy.*" *Kunapipi*, 11.2.(1989), p.101.

6  *Ibid.*, p.99.

7  *Ibid.*, p.101.

"a full and active participant in the history of her country" (*Sardines*, p.250) has the ring of "authorial approval".[8] For him her "status" has been uncomfortably "problematized" by the indeterminacy of her presentation. I think, however, that the structure of the novel provides the multiple, discordant perspectives on Medina which Wright finds damaging. Through these Farah succeeds where Achebe fell short, providing critical perspectives on salient contradictions and refusing to foreclose prematurely the conflict they engender.

Wright is not alone in objecting to the opendendedness and indeterminacy which characterize all of Farah's word. Matters of plot are left uncertain (Was Soyaan poisoned? Is Sagal pregnant?), motives are continually reexamined (why did Medina really leave Samater? Why is Mursal pursuing his kame-kaze mission? Why does Deeriye follow him?), and the ultimate value of this Group of Ten's resistence remains in question. Barbara Turfan wonders whether Farah is sufficiently cognizant of his characters' defects; if he is, why is he not more overtly judgmental of their inadequacies? Indeed, why not give us characters more adequate to the challenges they face? Part of my argument here is that Farah's refusal to give us characters who have resolved contradictions, his determination to present the contemporary situation in all its indeterminacy, contribute to his strength as a writer. I would further argue that critics like Wright and Turfan reflect an anti-modernist preference in readers of African literature, where modernism and indeterminacy are equated with an insufficiently committed position on the part of the writer. Achebe's Ikem, facing a version of this argument, says, "Writers don't give prescriptions.... They give headaches!" (*Anthills*, p.148). Farah has not shrunk from treating seriously the feminist challenge to patriarchy, nor has he made his presentation easier to come to terms with by giving us an unproblematic representative.

His presentation of Medina is in some ways similar to Virginia Woolf's of Clarissa Dalloway, both novelists refusing to resolve highly contradictory evaluations of their protagonists.

---

8 *Ibid.*, p.99.

However, there is this critical distinction in their works. The positive evaluation of Clarissa requires us to assent to a transcendental realm, outside time, wherein she communes with Septimus, her social opposite but spiritual companion. Only her capacity for a mysterious empathy with others saves Clarissa from being merely a society hostess. With Medina the positive and negative perspectives are located within history: the unresolved questions involve evaluating the efficacy of her actions in history, and this efficacy cannot yet be established. Thus the indeterminacy of Farah's novel keeps us engaged with historical process while Woolf's tempts us to escape it. It is important to see that the literary technique of modernism, critiqued by Lukacs as a decadent form of bourgeois evasion, can in fact work to quite different purposes in the African context. See also Neil Lazarus's similar argument about "the retrieval of naturalism" in African literature.

Judgments about good mothering obviously are grounded in judgments about the larger social context. Those who desire to adapt children to the world and those who prepare them to challenge it will certainly differ. Beyond this, good mothering involves the paradoxical effort to foster intimacy and autonomy, a balancing act which changes moment to moment and is hardly ever judged the same by two onlookers - or indeed by the participants themselves.

This issue of mothering is connected to our assessment of Medina's political gesture of leaving home. In both the domestic and public arenas, she claims that she acts to liberate others but is criticized for her egotistical desire to control. Her brother Nasser wonders whether she is not practising on Samater a policy not unlike the General's: "*Starve and rule*....Or had it all started with a small notion, with her saying that she wanted to change the position of a chair...the bed and other furniture...did she want to be the centre of everything?" (*Sardines*, p.103). Does Medina's effort to build a room of her own mean that

she has created a habitat in which she alone can function.[...] No room for either Samater or Ubax. [...] She put the chair in the wrong place in the dark. When Samater awoke, he stumbled on it and broke his neck" (*Sardines*, p.243).

Nasser's speculations become Xaddia's certainties: namely, that Medina is to blame for forcing Samater to oppose his mother and the General. Samater's sister Xaddia puts this accusation directly to Medina: "Tell me, then, What was the point of the charade in which Samater lost face and his job, my mother her son and dignity, Nasser and Dulman their freedom? What point have you made?" (*Sardines*, p.246). Xaddia's words support Wright's estimation of Medina's flamboyant, self-indulgent political gestures that hurt others and leave her unscathed. But hers are the anguished questions of a family member, close to someone in danger. It is appropriate that she should put the questions, and that we should have to weigh seriously the value of Medina's and others' resistance. There are, of course, responses to such questions. Medina thinks to herself: "If only Xaddia could understand that I'm fighting for the survivals of the woman in me, in her - while demolishing families like Idil's and regimes like the General's" (*Sardines*, p.246). Characterizing such language as Medina's "compulsive ideologizing", Wright ignores the tragic dilemmas which emerge in the women's argument: familial versus civic responsibilities, the intertwined threads of egoism and honor. Again taking his lead from Xaddia's accusations, Wright mistakenly blames Medina for the arrests of Dulman and Nasser, who are clearly presented in the text as independently engaged in different kinds of resistance. They, like Sagal's friends and perhaps even like Samater, are imprisoned in a general crackdown, which has nothing to do with Medina's departure except insofar as all are responses to the paranoid tyranny of the General. Wright's negative assessment of Medina's political acts depends partly on an assumption contradicted in the text.

Farah's trilogy focuses repeatedly on acts of resistance which are, in the short run, apparently futile. *Sardines* reflects the human condition: there are no positions outside of history from which we can judge with certainty the acts of others. There are only interested perspectives, on resistance as on mothering.

In offering a more positive perspective than Wright's on Medina, I have not wanted to present her as unquestionably heroic. Allusions and symbolic associations throughout the novel require us to see Medina in contradictory ways. Her name connects her to the holy city of the prophet's birth, "the city of righteousness" and to "Mina: the place where pillars are stoned, a symbol of Satan" (*Sardines*, p.146). She is associated throughout the novel with fire and with the figure of Prometheus, the demi-god whose contribution to a new order entailed his own extended torment. At the time of Medina's birth, a wing of her home was set on fire, perhaps by her dreadful grandfather, bent upon killing an unwanted female child. This circumstance connects her to another child who is burned to death, an event narrated in a chapter which offers the fullest treatment of the Promethean associations and extends their meaning from Medina to other women in the novel.

Farah's association of women with Prometheus - creator of humankind, bringer of fire, victim and rebel - suggests, at least, that they are not just midwives to history but actors in their own drama, narrators of their own lives, interpreters of their own dreams. Like Prometheus, they will figure as victims and rebels; they too will destroy and create. They will not escape the paradoxes of development nor easily resolve the contradictions deeply embedded within Somali society. Contrary to Achebe, Farah offers an image not of hope for the future but a representation of the complexity of the present - a complexity which, however else we read it, nevertheless authorizes Medina's claim to be "a full and active participant in the history of her country" (*Sardines*, p.250). That is what makes her, to borrow from Gordimer, "a true world-historical figure in Georg Lukacs's sense... one of the most extraordinary, attractive and moving women characters in any contemporary novel."

*Raoul Granqvist*

# MALE DISTANCE, FEMALE PROXIMITY:
## *ANTHILLS OF THE SAVANNAH* IN SCANDINAVIA

Chinua Achebe visited Scandinavia in October 1988, in view of two book launching ceremonies in Copenhagen and in Oslo. The Danish and the Norwegian translations of *Anthills of the Savannah*[1], appeared at this time. From Copenhagen and Oslo he was spurred to continue his tour to Sweden, where he met with readers of all kinds, students, academics, writers, and journalists. However, the Swedish translation of the novel was delayed, mainly because the major publishing companies that had been approached were not favourable to the text, for reasons that will emerge later.[2] The Swedish translation did not appear until September 1989, almost a year after his visit.[3]

The material premises of Achebe's critical reception in these three Scandinavian countries varied then, as Achebe himself was present in Denmark and Norway when the book was launched. The reception in these two countries was therefore much more unmediated and unmeditated, whereas the more substantial Swedish reception was intersected by several factors. One of these was the personal impact of Achebe himself, who visited the country a year prior to the publication of the book; of almost equal importance was the much longer history of his reputation in Sweden. In addition, a few of the reviews in Swedish (S1, F2, S2, S3, F3) were based on the English edition and appeared

---

1 Called Som vinden blaeser (Viborg: Samleren) respectively Nytt fra savannen (Drammen: J.W. Cappelens Forlag)

2 Achebe was interviewed by Folke Rydén on Swedish television (Rapport TV 2) on 21 October and asked what he thought about the delay. His answer was curt: "I do not mind it at all. I mean I would not read it in Swedish. It is for the Swedes to decide whether they want to read this story or not."

3 It was called *Termitstackarna pß savannen*. (Stockholm: Ordfronts förlag ).

before the Swedishtext was available. Moreover, some interviews (S4, S5, S14-16) were made during his visitto Sweden. These circumstantial differences did not change the direction of theScandinavian reception of the novel, but they probably had an impact on the way it wasformulated and on the preferences opted for.

A quantitative analysis of the material at hand reveals that Achebe scored equallywell in Denmark and Norway and that the Swedish reception, for reasons we have noted, wasmore penetrating and expansive. The press material can be divided into two main groups with Achebe's transactive part in it as the whetstone.[4]

The first, then, contains no direct mediation. The critics historicize the writer and his works in foregrounding terms, postulating Achebe as a colonized or a post-colonial writer, reinforcing dialectically the relative differences between us and them. The discourse reproduces earlier assumptions and suppositions about Achebe and African literature and filters them with the experiences emanating from the novel. It is critical in the two senses of the word. In the second group Achebe is both figuratively and literally present, interacting with the critic and the audience. The frame of reference of the latter group is the press conference or the interview, with the writer at the centre dominating both the direction and the mode of the discourse. We will first have a look at the last-mentioned interconnections.

Achebe gave a number of press conferences during his two-week Scandinavian tour, in Copenhagen, Oslo, Umeå, Uppsala, and Stockholm. The topics of these and the literary formulas he employed to project them did not vary in a considerable way. On each occasion he was motivated to dwell on his function as an increasingly alienated Nigerian social reformist and literary critic (D8, N2, N8), to expound patiently on the traditional truth saying rôle of the Igbo poet and writer and the lack of interest in *Anthills* (D5,D6, D9, N4), and lament bitterly the current political crises that exhaust the willpower of Nigeria, via intensified corruption

---

4 The cue within the parenthesis identifies the source. N: Norway; D: Denmark; S: Sweden; F: Finland. See the bibliography at the end.

and bad leadership (D6, D7, D8). Being asked to prognosticate about the future he frequently referred to the wisdom and guidance to befound in the final chapters of his book with their projection of the two model or ideal women, Beatrice and Elewa (D8, D9, D10, N3, S10). Naturally, these encounters with the Scandinavian media public, journalists, writers and students, also included elements of exchange and reciprocity. As the questions that he was asked were mostly diacritical and unspecific, Achebe found himself in a position where his talent for polemics and exegesis came in handy. From these encounters, then, Achebe - which is no surprise - emerged as the eloquent castigator of a type of neocolonialism in which the West is investing its energies and money to maintain control by proxies. His critique was twofold. The West would "let Africa go", abandon or retrench interest claims on loans as a political means of re-paying for centuries of robbery and deprivation; African leaders, in their turn, would have to "refocus" their responsibility and restore power to and engage their people. As indicated, he also had to respond to questions from people, mostly students, tho knew little or nothing about African literatures and African matters in general. His answers to questions about subjects such as négritude, his part in the Nigerian civil war, his choice of a secondary language for creative purposes, etc. were always candid and respectful.[5] Those critics who were present at these press conferences or had conducted individual interviews wrote about his novel from the perspective of what these encounters entailed. In their critique Achebe, the social critic and public figure, predominated decisively over the *Anthills* text.

However, in the following I will consider in some detail the viewpoints that one might infer were not mediated by the writer himself, but ensued out of "independent" readings of the novel. These sections of the reviews then constitute a discourse that is primarily involved with the text and less concerned with its social and ideological implications. This does not of course agree with

---

5 For a full report of these interviews, see my *Travelling: Chinua Achebe in Scandinavia. Swedish Writers in Africa*. [Umea Papers in English; 11], (Umea, 1990), pp. 25-42.

the aesthetic claims of Chinua Achebe's art, but this is not either what we are concerned about here. It provides insight into the structure ofthe Scandinavian reception of Achebe. It is here that one must look for its specifics.

Apart from Kole Omotoso's review of *Anthills*, published in the Norwegian *Morgounbladet* (N1) in November 1987, the only Scandinavian report on the book in the year of its appearance in English was by *Hufvudstadsbladet*'s (Finland) Kerstin Lindman-Stafford. She discussed the shortlisting of Achebe for the Booker McConell Prize and was convinced that he would win if the jury could appreciate his "distanced style of writing (F1)". I choose her cursory one-liner as emblematic of a discouraging, but clear, trend in the Scandinavian critique of Achebe's novel.

Many reviewers were unappreciative and critical of the conventions that the text is informed with. The shifts of narrative perspectives were seen as a burden on the reader. The switches from flashback technique to first-person narration, from monologue to dialogue, from British English to Pidgin, eventually distanced the western reader. They complicated and bewildered (N7, S2, S8, S21). "The writer has taken too much trouble, in a programmatic way," says one Swedish critic, "to incorporate all sorts of aspects, to involve all imaginable characters" (S12). He continues, however, saying apologetically that it is here that the real value of the novel lies; it is informative and illustrative. "It is definitely a treasure-house for the European who travels for the first time in Africa". The reluctance on the part of the Swedish publishers to bring out the translation lies here, I believe. The ideological and allegorical ramifications of the text, so much acclaimed, were not sustained and informed in the view of these readers by the narrative mode and structure. Content and form did not cooperate. The novel would do as a travel book or perhaps as a sociological document, but not as a novel. A few other examples confirm this lack of recognition of Achebe's employment of the post-colonial discourse. A Norwegian critic writes in his column that the book resembles an academic and uninspiring documentary report issued by Amnesty International (N9). And another adds that the story is passionless and light, "not at all for reflecting people" (N7). "I think I am watching a

Hollywood film that has received an Oscar", exclaims a Swedish critic who is equally repelled by the variations in narrative technique and thematic substance (S11). Achebe is admonished of being overtly didactic and sermonizing (S21); a suggestion that has a precedence in the 1960's criticism of his works.

When Achebe's novels first appeared in Scandinavia[6] in the late sixties he was hailed as an engaging documentalist and sociohistorian who told stories from an Africa that few knew about, but as a literary artist in his own category he fared pretty badly.[7] There are reminiscences, as we have seen, of the same colonial discourse in the latter-day readings of him. Yet, we must hasten to add, these voices are few and increasingly divided. The great majority of them are very positive. One or two of our respondents in fact judge Achebe as one of world literature's chief innovators of style and language and group him with writers such as Anita Desai, Salmon Rushdie, and Randolph Stow (D1). Seeing the overall criticism of him reflected against the transmissive history of western criticism of Achebe and its Scandinavian imprints one cannot but notice the changes that have taken place since the late sixties when his earlier novels appeared in Scandinavia.

The critics base their opinions of *Anthills* on a variety of persuasions. There are frequent references, as one might guess, to his Igbo background and aesthetics (D3, S1,F2, S23); to the political realism motivating and sympathysing the text and its employment of the contemporary Nigerian situation (S7, S19); to its syncretism and polyvocality, to its postmodernistic slant (D4), to, in fact, its merging of realism and psychology, its hopefulness and faith in the range and capacity of the human voice (S18,S22).

But the new alliances that *Anthills* projects between men and women, between women and women, between ethnic and social groups, in short the novel's reformist cultural poetics, are the

---

6  *Things Fall Apart* has been translated into Danish, Norwegian, and Swedish, *No Longer at Ease* into Danish only, *A Man of the People* into Danish, Norwegian, Swedish and Finnish; *Arrow of God* has not been translated into any of these langauges.

7  Raoul Granqvist: "The Early Swedish Reviews of Chinua Achebe's Things Fall Apart and A Man of the People", *Research in African Literatures* 15 (1984), 394-404.

factors that the critics elaborate most of all (D3, D9, N3, N6, N8, F3, S9, S10). The best critical writing on *Anthills* is to be found here. On this subject, particularly insightful and perceptive are the reviews written by Scandinavian women critics (D2, D4,D8, D10, S20, S23). In fact, this is the first time that a sustained women's reading of Achebe has materialised in Scandinavia. They foreground Beatrice's erotic *cum* spiritual vitality and associate it with an ideal form of responsible leadership. The protagonist's affinity with Achebe himself as a universal storyteller and cultural mediator is also accounted for (D10.)[8]

Chinua Achebe's *Anthills of the Savannah* was not met with the same public fervour in Scandinavia as when his earlier novels came out. There are at least two reasons for this. One is that their publication largely coincided with the tragic events leading up to the Nigerian civil war. They were projected and read as timely witnesses to the collapse of colonialized Africa and telling evidence of rifts in the new structure. Their popularity must also be explained as a characteristic of the widening concerns of the time for the world outside. Studies of African literature were just to begin. The scenario for the reception of *Anthills* is another: Africa is no longer a continent that needs to be explained; many of her writers are well-known to a fairly large readership; Achebe himself is studied at many levels in school and at university. His readership is also expanding, including more women readers. However, the rather timid, although qualified, response to *Anthills* resonates here and there with echoes from the imperial context. There is still homework to be done.

---

8  For Achebe's readings, lectures, and comments on various aspects of women, see *Travelling*, pp. 1-18, 47.

# BIBLIOGRAPHY

## Danish reviews

D1  Lars Ole Sauerberg: "Diktatur i Afrika" ("African Dictatorship").
    *Morgonavisen. Jyllands Posten.* 5 January 1988.
D2  Marianne Madelung: "Magtens anatomi" ("The Anatomy of Power").
    *Politiken.* 8 March 1988.
D3  Knud Vilby: "En roman fra Afrikas smerteligt dunkende hjerte" ("A
    Novel from Africa's Beating Heart"). *Information.* 22 September 1988.
D4  Grethe Røstbøll: "Stor afrikansk roman" ("A Great African Novel").
    *Morgenavisen. Jyllands Posten.* 27 September 1988.
D5  Jens Kerte: "Afrikansk roman om makt og korruption" ("African Novel
    about Powerand Corruption"). *Politiken.* 18 October 1988.

D6   Svend Thaning: "Manden der ikke fik nobel prisen" ("The Man Who Did Not Receive the Novel Prize"). *Berlingske Tidende.* 18 October 1988.

D7   Gitte Redder: "Nye begydnelser kraever nye ledere" ("New Beginnings Require New Leaders"). *Kristeligt Dagblad.* [18] October 1988.

D8   Karen Syberg and Peter Wivel: "Jag kender selv Afrikas problemer -jeg behøver ikke Vestens belaering" ("I know the Problems of Africa: I Don't Need to Be Taught by the West"). *Information.* 21 October 1988.

D9   Bo Bjørnvig: "Løj man, død man!" ("If You Lie, You Are Dead"). *Weekendavisen Berlingske Aften.* 21 October 1988.

D10  Marianne Madelung: "Kunstner ved religøst ombud" ("The Artist as a Religous Mediator"). *Politiken.* 26 October 1988.

## Norwegian reviews

N1   Kole Omotoso: "En bevisst nigeriansk roman" ("A Special Nigerian Novel"), *Morgonbladet.* [November 1987].

N2   Finn Jor: "Vår siste sjanse" ("Our Last Chance"). *Aftenposten.* 17 October 1988.

N3   Svein Johs Ottesen: "Fyrsten og skalden - i Afrika" ("The Poet and the Emperor - in Africa"). *Aftenposten.* 18 October 1988.

N4   Sverre M. Nyrønning: "En verden av smerte" ("A World of Pain"). *Adresseavisen.* 20 October 1988".

N5   Turid Larsen: "Klart för bokfesten" (Ready for the bookfair"). *Arbeiderbladet.* 29 September 1988.

N6   Janne Kjellberg: "Nytt fra Achebe" ("New Things by Achebe"). *Klassekampen.* 12 October 1988.

N7   Karl Richarad Thuve: "Ted og spennende om maktkamper" ("Solid and Exciting about the Power Struggle"). *Vart land.* 19 [26] October 1988.

N8   Helge Rønning: "Maktens spill i Afrika" ("The African Power Game"). *Dagbladet.* 28 October 1989.

N9   Kjell Oloaf Jensen: "Overflatisk om tyranniet" ("A Shallow Description of Tyranny"). *Arbeiderbladet.* 7 December 1988.

## Reviews in Swedish

F1   Kerstin Lindman-Strafford: "Booker eller inte Booker" ("Booker or not Booker"). *Hufvudstadsbladet.* 9 October 1987.

S1   Raoul Granqvist: "Afrikans skildring av tiden människans boning" ("An African's Description of Time - the Habitat of Man"). *Västerbottens Folkblad.* 3 August 1988.

F2   Raoul Granqvist: "Tiden är människans boning" ("Time is the Habitat of Man"). *Hufvudstadsbladet.* 11 August 1988.

S2    Jöran Mjöberg: "Despotin demaskerad - Achebes romankonst" ("Tyranny Demasked _Achebe's Art"). *Svenska Dagbladet*. 16 September 1988. See also anon. "Fotnoten. Ny dag. Chinua Achebe" ("The Footnote. A New Day: Chinua Achebe"). *Sveriges Dagblat*. 22.9. 1989. Ref. to Mjöberg's article.

S3    Raoul Granqvist: "[Chinua Achebe] en gudabenådad berättare" ([Chinua Achebe]: A Divine Storyteller"). *Västerbottens-Kuriren*. 31 October 1988.

F3    Raoul Granqvist: "[Chinua Chebe]. berättare och samhällskritiker" (["ChinuaAchebe]: Storyteller and Critic"). *Vasabladet*. 11 December 1988.

S4    Janet Suslick: "Chinua Achebe på besök i Umeå: ` Som om Strindberg äkte till Nigeria" ("Chinua Achebe Visiting Umeå: ` As If Strindberg Went to Nigeria"'). *Västerbottens Folkblad*. 21 October 1988.

S5    Leif Larsson: "En försoningens röst i Afrika: [Chinua Achebe], 'Rasismen Europas Dystra arv"' ("An African Voice Of Redemption. [Chinua Achebe]: 'Racism: Europe's Grim Heritage"'). *Västerbottens-Kuriren*. 22 October 1988.

S6    Raoul Granqvist: "Chinua Achebe, Afrikas mest lästa författare. ,Jag var en dansandevilde..." ("Chinua Achebe, the Most-Read African Writer: 'I Was a Dancing Savage..."'). *Om* 4: 1989, 3-4

S7    Karl Steinick: "Stigen måste ständigt röjas" ("The Path Has to Be Constantly Cleared"). *Helsingfors Dagblad*. 1 October 1989.

S8    Leif Risberg: "Chinua Achebe. Åter efter 20 år. Infriar inga förväntiningar" ("Chinua Achebe is Back after Twently Years. Does Not Meet the Expectations"). *Ö Corr*. 19 October 1989.

S9    "Nya böcker" ("New Books"). *Bokfönstret*. *Sveriges Radio*. 16 October 1989.

S10   Per Wästberg: "Thriller full av död" ("A Thriller Filled with Death"). *Dagens Nyheter*. 10 January 1990.

S11   Carl-Erik Nordberg: "En genomskådare av förtryckets mekanismer" ("He Reveals the Mechanisms of Suppression"). *Arbetet*. 15 December 1989.

S12   Lennart Hagerfors: "Tvärsnitt gbenom yttervärlden" ("A Slice of the World"). *Bonniers Litterära Magasin* 5:58 (1989), 325.

S13   Jan Ristarp: "Kvinnan som ger hopp om värdigare framtid" ("The Woman that Gives Hope about a More Dignified Future"). *SDS* 3 February 1990.

S14   Thomas Polvall: "Chinua Achebe, författare från Nigeria: 'För att skriva sanningenkrävs mod"' ("Chinua Achebe, a Writer from Nigeria: 'To Write about Truth You Have to Be Courageous"'). *HD*. 30.10.1988

90

S15  Thomas Polvall: "Chinua Achebe, Nigeria: 'Jag försökte återskapa den förlorade identiteten"' ("Chinua Achebe, Nigeria: 'I Tried to Recuperate my Lost Identity"'). *ST*. 31.10.1988. The same as 14.

S16  Thomas Polvall: "Historierna väntade på att bli berättade" ("The Stories WereThere to Be Told"). *NSD*. 7.11.1988. the same as 14.

S17  Erik Östling: Review of "Termitstackarna. (A Review article). *Bibliotekstjönst AB*. 8.11.1989. Also includes a review by Kerstin Sinha of the English edition.

S18  Kersti Bergold: "Achebe målar Afrika svart. Komplex största synden" ("Achebe Paints Africa Black: Inferiority the Greatest Sin"). *VLT* 24.10.1989.

S19  Ingrid Björkman: "Achebes återkomst" ("Achebe's Return"). *GP* 28.11.1989.

S20  Monica Lauritzen: "Med det folkliga som rötter..." ("[Achebe's] Roots are in the Countryside"). *GT* 9.11.1989.

S21  Keith Millom: "Romanen som tangerar verklighetet" ("The Novel that is Close to Reality"). *NWT*. 22.11.1989.

S22  Thomas Polvall: "Den genomhederlige blev en maktberusad odugling" ("The Honest Man Who Became Intoxicated with Power"). *NSD*. 22.11.1989.

S23  Suzanne Unell: "Emotsedd Achebe" ("A Much-Longed-For Achebe"). *NA*. 13.12.1989.

*Joachim Schultz[1]*

# ENTRETIEN AVEC ZAMENGA BATUKEZANGA

## Introduction

On ne trouve pas souvent le nom de Zamenga Batukezanga dans les études sur la littérature zaïroise. Rouch et Clavreuil ne lui consacrent pas de chapitre entier dans leur anthologie *Littératures nationales d'écriture française.*[2] Ils le mentionnent seulement dans l'introduction du chapitre sur la littérature zaïroise:

> Zamenga Batukezanga est un des seuls à s'être exprimés exclusivement en prose avec huit récits ou romans entre 1971 et 1979: citons *Souvenirs du village* (1971), *Les Hauts et les Bas* (1971), *Bandoki, les sorciers* (1973), *Carte postale* (1974).

Avec cela, ils font allusion à la riche production littéraire de Zamenga, figure populaire qu'on appelle avec sympathie à Kinshasa "Papa Zamenga".

Si l'on analysait ses livres d'après nos critères européen, il faudrait sans doute parler de *Trivialliteratur* - littérature des masses. Zamenga est un romancier du peuple qui a beaucoup de succès au Zaïre. Ses oeuvres sont tous parus aux Editions Saint-Paul qui publient surtout des livres de religion et d'édification. Ces livres sont bon marchés, ce qui implique leur extérieur modeste. Zamenga écrit sur la vie quotidienne, ses thèmes vont des problèmes conjugaux à la sorcellerie. La structure narrative joue pour lui un rôle secondaire, il raconte ses histoires comme les gens simples de son public les auraient racontées eux-mêmes.

---

1  Propos recueillis par Joachim Schultz, Kinshasa le 5 avril 1989. Publié ici avec des remerciements pour M. Mühlschlegel, l'ancien directeur du Goethe-Institut Kinshasa.
2  Alain Rouch/Gérard Clavreuil: *Littératures nationales d'écriture française. Afrique noire. Caraïbes. Océan Indien.* (Paris 1986).

Ainsi, il s'adapte à leur goût, et quelques-uns de ses livres sont déjà parus en deuxième édition.

En 1989, il a fondé sa propre maison d'édition, ZABAT, pour ne plus être soumis aux contraintes de son éditeur catholique, bien qu'il ait eu assez de liberté. Comme il avait les possibilités de voyager, il s'est rendu aux Etats-Unis, au Canada et en Allemagne fédérale. Il a publié ses impressions de voyage sous forme de lettres à sa femme dans son livre *Chérie Basso*.[3] Le pédagogue et journaliste zaïrois Djungu-Simba Kamatenda, qui a publié aussi des livres pour enfants, écrit dans la préface de ce roman épistolaire:

> Zamenga sorcier? Naïf? Superstitieux? - Méfiez-vous en. Sous ses airs de naïveté apparente, à travers ses histoires manifestement drôles et invraisemblables parfois, l'auteur distille son message. Suivant la bonne vieille pédagogie africaine, il instruit en amusant. C'est, en somme, sa façon de créer la fiction.[4]

---

3    *Chérie Basso*, 1983, 2e édition 1989.
4    *Ibid.* pp. 9, 10

*Joachim Schultz*: En ce moment, on parle assez souvent de la littérature néo-africaine, mais il faut dire que la littérature du Zaïre n'est pas tellement connue. Vous êtes un des auteurs zaïrois les plus connus. Comment voyez-vous votre rôle d'écrivain dans ce pays et dans ce monde aussi?

*Zamenga Batukazenga*: Je ne me rendais pas compte de tout mon rôle; je n'ai fait qu'écrire. Mais plus j'écris, plus il y a une sorte de communication qui se fait, et je ne m'attendais pas à ce terme "acte" de l'écriture. Parce que c'est ce qu'on a toujours négligé dans le temps et même maintenant puisqu'on croit que le développement c'est d'abord la technologie, et on oublie l'Homme. Nous avons connu beaucoup de choses en Afrique en général, où on introduit une technique, mais tout à fait comme un rejet du coeur.
Mais dans tout le peuple on s'accroche à l'essence donc aux fondements; et ces fondements, c'est quoi? Les croyances, les mythes, tout ce qui est religion, les religions africaines et la conception que l'Afrique s'est fait du monde, l'interprétation que l'Africain fait du monde. Je me rends compte qu'un Allemand est différent de moi, un Américain, un Chinois - mais pour aller voir cela, il faut avoir des références. Chaque fois que je vois quelque chose en Allemagne, en Union Soviétique, pour le comprendre, je me réfère à ma culture. Qu'est-ce que cela signifie? Donc l'homme a toujours une référence de chez lui pour interpréter ce qu'il voit de nouveau.

*Schultz*: De sa propre tradition?

*Zamenga*: Oui, et tout ça ensemble. Alors, pour moi, c'est très important et maintenant, après 30 ans d'indépendance de l'Afrique, je crois que tout le monde s'accorde à dire: "on dirait qu'on recule". Pourquoi on recule? Justement, l'éducation que nous avons reçu pendant un certain temps nous a appris à mépriser le milieu dans lequel on vit. Or il est impossible à un individu de se développer s'il ne part pas de son milieu. Or on vous dira de la colonisation; il n'y a pas toujours que des mauvais. Je peux peut-être revenir maintenant à ce qu'il y a de bon dans la colonisation. Je ne parle même plus de colonisation, je parle de rencontre de cultures. Ces rencontres de cultures peuvent avoir de différentes formes, parfois des formes violentes, et peut-être la colonisation peut être située dans la violence des rencontres, ou bien dans l'amitié comme nous faisons comme ça.

*Schultz*: Dans votre roman *Sept frères et une soeur,*[5] vous parlez du thème du suicide. Le suicide n'était pas connu dans les sociétés traditionnelles africaines. Est-ce que vous voulez dire par ce roman que le suicide est entré dans la société africaine par le contact avec une autre culture, par le colonialisme?

*Zamenga*: Le suicide, c'est quoi? Moi, je crois que le suicide n'est pas le fait de se tuer nécessairement. Ce n'est qu'un résultat. Le vrai suicide que nous vivons tous, c'est justement le fait d'être rejeté de la communauté. Lorsque l'individu est rejeté de la communauté, il est perdu, il est inutile. Alors ce phénomène-là s'est accentué avec la rencontre violente des deux cultures. Parce qu'ici, il y a d'abord la communauté africaine qui veut que tout le monde soit pour l'individu, que l'individu ne s'écarte pas, en tous cas ne soit pas dans la misère.
C'est pourquoi vous verrez que, dans la culture, il était très difficile de concevoir l'orphelinat. Tout le monde est père et mère. Et dans la société moderne: ça craque. Seul, vous êtes incapable, on vous dira. Vous savez qu'à l'école vous avez échoué, on vous le dit, alors que dans la société traditionnelle, on ne vous dira pas que vous avez échoué. On vous encourage toujours à participer à la société. Ici, vous avez un échec, vous vous mariez, obligatoire, vous allez à la messe, vous ne vous entendez pas avec votre femme, l'église...

*Schultz*: Alors dans ce roman, c'est plutôt à un niveau symbolique?

---

5    Kinshasa: Editions St. Paul, 1983.

*Zamenga*: Symbolique, oui. Mais sinon, le symbole, le fondement, c'est l'emprise du matériel sur l'homme; et puisque tout le monde court vers le matériel, celui qui ne court pas est inutile. Alors il y a suicide. Et donc, ça s'accentue maintenant en Afrique, le suicide. Surtout avec l'argent, avec la réussite, l'échec, et ainsi de suite. Mais il y a un aspect que je suis en train d'étudier: il y a des gens qui se suicidaient dans la société en pensant que...

*Schultz*: Dans la société moderne ou traditionnelle?

*Zamenga*: Traditionnelle. Le suicide semble que ça a perdu de sa valeur. Parce que fondamentalement, à un moment donné, quand un vieux voit qu'il est à la charge des autres, et que les autres s'occupent de lui, et que les autres n'ont plus de liberté, et que tout le monde doit s'occuper de lui, il dit: "Mais pourquoi je dois exister si c'est pour entraver la liberté des autres?".

*Schultz*: Dans votre roman *Bandoki*,[6] vous parlez plutôt de la société traditionnelle et de la sorcellerie. Est-ce que la sorcellerie joue toujours un rôle aussi important dans la société moderne africaine?

*Zamenga*: C'est regrettable, mais on n'a jamais été sincère dans ces histoires. Eh bien, curieusement, la sorcellerie joue encore un rôle plus important que jamais. Et chez qui? Chez les occidentalisés, chez des intellectuels, la forme a changé. En Afrique, même au niveau le plus haut, qui n'a pas son marabout?

*Schultz*: Mais il faut dire, d'autre part, qu'il y a aussi des formes de sorcellerie dans les sociétés de l'ouest. C'est-à-dire, qu'il y a des chiffres magiques, des signes dans la vie: on dit par exemple, qu'un chat noir venant de gauche porte malheur. Alors, ça existe partout.

---

6    Kinshasa: Editions St. Paul, 1973.

*Zamenga*: Ici, c'est curieux, mais il y a vraiment l'homme qui vit le moment le plus dramatique en Afrique, c'est l'intellectuel africain. Il vit un drame parce qu'il ne se libère pas encore d'une société comme de l'autre. Il est pris dans l'engrenage de la société moderne occidentalisée qu'il ne maîtrise pas, où il ne se sent pas totalement à l'aise. Mais il n'entre pas totalement dans la société.

*Schultz*: J'aimerais revenir encore à cet autre roman, *Sept frères*. Il commence comme un conte: "Il y avait jadis..."; et le titre aussi me rappelle les contes: *Sept frères*. Dans les contes allemands, il y a beaucoup de contes où on parle de sept frères qui, par exemple, se transforment en sept corbeaux. Le chiffre sept a pour nous un sens magique. Est-ce que le conte est, pour ce roman, et pour d'autres de vos romans, un modèle?

*Zamenga*: Dans la narration,oui. Vous voyez, les écrivains africains, jusqu'à présent, ont un complexe de vouloir s'assimiler au style occidental. L'effort que j'ai fait, c'est d'être plus près de l'oralité, parce que l'oralité, c'est ce qu'il y a de plus vivant. Alors, quand j'écris, contrairement à ce qu'on peut me reprocher. On dit: "Ah! oui, il écrit comme il parle". Et pour moi, c'est une fierté quand j'apprends que j'écris comme je parle, parce que l'écrit est une substitution.

*Schultz*: C'est aussi pour mieux atteindre le public?

*Zamenga*: Maintenant, avec la télévision, nous revenons à l'oralité. Donc j'essaie quand même de changer ce style-là, du village près de l'oralité. Mais je prends par exemple ... quand vous avez *Lettres d'Amérique*, ou bien *Chérie Basso*, le voyage que j'ai effectué en Allemagne, ça, ce sont des lettres. Mais c'est l'astuce aussi. Je m'adresse à ma femme, mais en fait à la femme africaine en lui présentant tout ce que je vois à l'étranger, en comparant ce qui se fait chez nous à ce que je suis en train de voir et pour quels renseignements on peut en tirer. Alors ça, c'est encore une autre forme. Ou bien la forme, par exemple, de "Sommes sur le fleuve Zaïre." Bon, là, poésie, mais ce n'est pas de la poésie à l'occidentale, où il faut rimer. Il ne faut pas rimer des mots. Non, moi, c'est l'émotion, mais l'émotion qui part des contes, des mythes, etc. Vous voyez, les mythes qui peuvent se vérifier à nos jours.

*Schultz*: Alors, on pourrait dire que la base de votre écriture, c'est l'émotion? Et vous le transformez en écriture?

*Zamenga*: Oui. Et c'est difficile pour moi, parce que l'émotion, je peux l'avoir plutôt dans ma langue maternelle.

*Schultz*: Quelle est votre langue maternelle?

*Zamenga*: Le kikongo. C'est une des langues anciennes, mais maintenant, avec le problème des échanges politiques, c'est une langue qui se perd de plus en plus au profit du lingala. Mais en fait, disons tout simplement que le problème de l'Africain, c'est l'émotion d'abord. Dans l'émotion, c'est l'inspiration, c'est l'inspiration qui me guide. Lorsque je vois qu'il y a un personnage qui arrive en tête avec ses problèmes, je fais en sorte d'être fidèle à cette émotion-là. Et ce n'est qu'après que je me rends compte que je suis en train d'écrire aux gens, aux personnes. Mais c'est la vie quotidienne.

*Schultz*: Comme ça, vous atteignez le public. Justement, vous écrivez en français, quel est le contact avec le public?

*Zamenga*: Quand j'écris, la première chose, c'est l'émotion. C'est tant pis pour le public. D'abord, c'est le public de ce personnage, mais il se fait que, quand c'est publié, tout le monde se retrouve, des jeunes comme des vieux. Mais surtout les jeunes de 18 à 20-25 ans.

*Schultz*: C'est plutôt un public jeune que vous avez?

*Zamenga*: Oui. C'est parce qu'il y avait un développement historique: le public agé n'a pas été instruit: c'est une raison. Alors le public universitaire a été, depuis 25 ans, 20 ans, l'objet de débats sur le style Zamenga. Ça n'a pas été admis de prime abord. Et les gens, les autres ont voulu écrire comme les Français. Et le public n'accepte pas. Moi, j'essaie de prendre l'émotion, de l'exprimer dans le langage commun. Parce que ce sont des préoccupations communes à toutes les générations. Alors, je prends le langage de la rue, et il y en a qui prennent ça sous un angle péjoratif. Mais la rue n'est pas du tout pour moi quelque chose de péjoratif: c'est là où il y a du vrai.

*Schultz*: Alors vous cherchez aussi vos thèmes, vos sujets dans la vie quotidienne?

*Zamenga*: Oui. Dans la vie de la rue, quand je sors, je regarde; une fois, une femme enceinte qui marche difficilement; un type qui tombe, le bus, les problèmes, en tous cas les préoccupations, la faim, les injustices que je vois: vraiment la vie quotidienne telle qu'elle est vécue comme préoccupation de l'ensemble de l'humanité. Il faut que ça coule, et qu'on ne laisse passer aucun aspect de la vie. C'est ça; sinon j'aurais bien voulu être vraiment cinéaste. Mais j'aimerais plutôt que les autres exploitent mon oeuvre. Mais ce que je fais pour que tout le monde puisse comprendre, c'est des bandes dessinées. Le même thème, la même préoccupation, la même lecture, partagées en plusieurs sections, pour que tout le monde puisse y avoir accès. Et c'est ainsi que maintenant, il y a des bandes dessinées; il y a un thème écrit, mais je le mets en bande dessinée, comme ça même les illettrés disent: "Ah! Ça, et ça, et ça..."

*Schultz*: Ça existe déjà, vos textes en bandes dessinées?

*Zamenga*: Oui, on en a fait. Nous publions sous forme de recueil. J'ai 14 recueils reprenant la topographie des préoccupations des Africains à partir de la tradition. Nous sommes à collectionner ça chez St. Paul. On l'a intitulé: "La pierre qui saigne". Vous voyez que la culture africaine est en train de saigner. Mais quand on aura terminé le texte, le même texte, on le reprend sous forme de bande dessinée. La plupart des livres sont comme ça.

*Schultz*: Comment est le contact avec l'édition St. Paul?

*Zamenga*: Vous voyez, l'édition en Afrique est quelque chose d'inimaginable. C'est difficile à trouver un éditeur comme ça se passe en Europe. Quand vous écrivez, que vous voulez diffuser les images de l'Afrique, de la vie africaine, et si l'édition est en Europe, on ne rendra pas le texte de la même manière. On voudra plutôt que vous transformiez les images aux images africaines pour le public européen. Moi-même, je me perds dans cette histoire. Parce que je sais que ce ne sont pas les images que je voudrais présenter; surtout, je sais que l'Africain ne se retrouvera pas là-bas. Deuxièmement, le livre ne reviendra pas au Zaïre. S'il revient, il va coûter 10 ou 20 fois plus cher.

Alors, une fois que vous avez fait ça, quel est l'éditeur? Ici, en Afrique, ça n'existe pas. Vous envoyez en Europe, et on vous dit: "On a modifié tout ça." Mais si je modifie, c'est ma mort à moi. Alors c'était dur. J'écrivais toujours comme ça, je commençais à publier à compte d'auteur; le premier livre, le deuxième livre à compte d'auteur, c'était dur.

La maison St. Paul a quelque chose d'original. Comme ils sont ici, en Afrique, ils ont dit: "Ce qui nous intéresse, ce sont les préoccupations des africains. C'est-à-dire que les livres que nous avons faits ici ne doivent pas avoir la même forme qu'en Europe. Et pour cela, il faut chercher les auteurs qui peuvent exprimer l'âme africaine. Seulement eux, et pas ceux-là." Alors ils ont fait d'abord une revue. On m'a demandé, parce que j'écrivais dans les journaux, si je pouvais collaborer à cette revue-là. Eh bien j'ai fait le premier livre, *Les hauts et les bas* (1971), et ça a eu un succès fou, c'est simple, les gens attendaient à la porte. J'ai dit: "Mais on fait un livre", et depuis ce moment là, St. Paul publie des romans qui sont conformes à son action, sa philosophie catholique.

Tandis que les textes qui ne sont pas conformes à sa philosophie, moi je les ai, on me les renvoie. Il faut rester un peu dans la philosophie de St. Paul, mais dans la mesure où St. Paul respecte ma Philosophie, et vice-versa. Quand ça ne répond pas, quand on change la forme de mon texte, je le reprends. J'ai pas moins de 8 textes qui me sont renvoyés.

*Schultz*: Pensez-vous que c'est plus important de publier ici qu'à l'étranger?

*Zamenga*: Oui. La mission de l'écrivain, je crois. Même s'il faut faire connaître l'Afrique, c'est ici que nous présenterons la vraie Afrique, et nos amis viendront, auront l'intérêt de nous découvrir. Mais si nous falsifions la pensée africaine pour simplement plaire à l'extérieur - c'est fini.

*Chantal Zabus*[1]

# OF TORTOISE, MAN AND LANGUAGE.
# AN INTERVIEW WITH GABRIEL OKARA

*Chantal Zabus*: Gabriel Okara, you wrote one novel[2] and another one has been known to be in the making for five or six years. You write poetry and short stories, and you are now, late in your career, it seems, tackling a new genre - children's literature. How do you define yourself? As a novelist, a poet? Or have you been writing children's literature all the time?

*Gabriel Okara*: I think I am a poet first. I wouldn't describe myself as a novelist. The thought of writing for children has always been in me. We don't have a reading habit. Only in the classroom situation are people taught English and are given certain recommended books to read; not for enjoyment and that's what fiction should be read for. That's why our readings are limited to recommended books for exams and things like that but not for entertainment. One should start with the young, write stories for the young, as supplementary readers both inside and outside the classroom.
My books are sold at motor-parks and markets and are recommended for all schools in Rivers State by the Government.

*Zabus*: Are they selling much better than poems and short stories, say?

*Okara*: Oh sure! Definitely. Children, when they see me in the street, they say: "Ah, that's the Little Snake and Little Frog-writer"... you know, that makes me happy.

*Zabus*: When did you actually start writing for children?

---

1   This interview was held at the University of Kent, Canterbury, on August 27, 1989.
2   *The Voice*. (London: Heinemann, 1964). [African Writers Series]

*Okara*: As a matter of fact, it was the Government in Rivers State that commissioned me. The Governor and I used to talk about the need for children's books reflecting our culture for our children before he became Governor. "Let us now put in practice what we used to talk about," he said; "Look, I don't want writers to starve. Come and see me and let's talk about it." I went and the result was my being commissioned to write books for children as we had talked about.

*Zabus*: And what about the writing of short stories. Is that something that you have been doing for quite a while, throughout your career?

*Okara*: Yes, even before the publication of The Voice. That's what I wrote first and I won the first prize in the Eastern Region's 1952 short story competition organized by the British Council.

*Zabus*: Critics have said that African writers, particularly South African writers, of short stories are in fact short-distance performers. What do you make of that? Did you first start writing short stories because it is an easy genre, short and dense, as a way, perhaps, of preparing for The Voice, which would be longer?

*Okara*: No, it is much more difficult to write short stories than a novel. It is restricted, a particular form that is condensed. I used to compare it to a musical form, a short form of musical composition, the concerto, not as long as a symphony. In poetry, the equivalent would be a sonnet; it is more controlled. To write a sonnet is more difficult than writing a longer poem.

*Zabus*: So it is easier when you have a lot of narrative space at your disposal?

*Okara*: Yes, that is right. A short story is much more concentrated, more difficult. It has room for only the essentials and follows strictly the rules.

*Zabus*: So the poem then is even more difficult because it is a shorter unit? Is it not a matter of hierachizing difficulty, the novel being the easiest, then the short story, then the poem?

*Okara*: No, it depends on the writer. I find certain things easier to express in prose than in a poem.

*Zabus*: I see. Do you remember the first poem that you ever wrote? And, by contrast, do you remember the first poem that was published? Are these two the same?

*Okara*: No, the first poem I wrote was never published. That was in Lagos, during the early years of the Second World War. I lost it.

*Zabus*: Your poetry has been said to be influenced by Gerald Manley Hopkins - Nigerian critic Theo Vincent mentioned this. Did Hopkins influence you?

*Okara*: Of course, he did. I like his concept of inscape. What you see is not it. There is something behind what you see. The essence of man, tree or mountain. They are telling us things which the casual looker misses. There is a human form I can see looking at you now. But the essential self is what you do not see; it is the spirit.

*Zabus*: In Hopkins' work, there is the "sprung rhythm" in the prosody of his poetry; there are double or even triple-barrelled coinages, there is a stringing, a linking of words together and hyphenating them. We find this both in Hopkins' poetry and yours. So do they come from Ijo,[3] do they condense Ijo thought or do they come from Hopkins?

---

3 Ijo, a language spoken in the South-Eastern part of Nigeria, is Okara's native language.

*Okara*: I think both. Because in Ijo, too, we describe things in that sort of way. For example, in Ijo, "Karu karu sei torumo," which would translate literally into "Red-bad eyes."

*Zabus*: In Hopkins' poetry, Latin is latent, just like Ijo would be in yours. It would be interesting to compare them, for Latin is a dead or at least a creolized language and Ijo is a minor language threatened with extinction.

*Okara*: No, Ijo is alive and thriving.

*Zabus*: Do you expect it to be living and thriving for a long time?

*Okara*: Yes, I think so. It is the fourth registered language in Nigeria.

*Zabus*: So, you don't feel it is going to be crushed like some other Nigerian languages which are not faring as well as Ijo? Do you think they will always be thriving?

*Okara*: You see, 80 per cent of Nigerians live in the rural areas and in those rural areas, indigenous languages are spoken and are thriving. What you say about the extinction of smaller languages may perhaps happen in the urban areas but not in the rural areas.

*Zabus*: Not in the rural areas, but if there is a major exodus, as there has been, from the villages to the urban centres?

*Okara*: That is being discouraged by establishing infrastructures and industries so that people stay in the rural areas. Some people from various tribal groups who were born and educated in the urban areas don't speak their own languages. Take Lagos, for instance, many people speak Yoruba. I know some Ijo people who don't speak their language; they don't understand it at all; they speak Yoruba or English. In some other urban areas, they speak only English in one form or another. This is true of not only Ijos but others as well, particularly the middle class urban-dwellers. If we examine how the English language has insinuated itself into the very core of the life of various, important and articulate segments of our society, we find that to this segment of our society, the middle-class, English is no longer an alien language. To them and many more, English has become a de facto-African language. It seems to me that when a native language becomes a conscious activity, it has lost its premier position to another which comes more easily and naturally to your lips. The urban middle-class dwellers and the other less affluent but who are also urban dwellers have thus become speakers of some form of the English language in preference to their native languages. They only speak their native languages, some haltingly, others only when absolutely necessary.

Such an outcome predictably is inevitable when many children of middle-class urban dwellers attend special expatriate schools. In these schools, the girls are taught to curtsey and the boys to bow from the waist up with a flourish of the right hand holding a top hat with the elegance of Elizabethan ladies and gentlemen.

*Zabus*: Even now?

*Okara*: Yes, they are even taught to dance ballet. The so-called high class schools. This is not exactly what is happening now ...

*Zabus*: But it is a caricature of what they are doing now. Well, to go back to Ijo. Let us take the reader of Little Snake and Little Frog - this reader speaks both Ijo and English. But is he or she educated in Ijo; is Ijo a medium of instruction in the school?

*Okara*: No, that book that I have written is not only for Ijos; it is for all Nigerian children; it is for all children in Rivers State and all other states.

*Zabus*: But is Ijo a medium of instruction in the school?

*Okara*: No, not yet.

*Zabus*: Would you wish it to be? Do you think it would create problems because it is in direct competition with English and it would be one at the expense of the other?

*Okara*: Even if one wanted to, there are almost no teachers to teach Ijo. This is true of many languages in Nigeria. It is only recently that they have been making attempts in the rural Ijo area to teach Ijo in elementary schools. The teaching of Nigerian languages in schools is being made a national policy. We, in our time, we did a bit of Ijo, to read and write Ijo. Not very much, but that has enabled us to read and write a bit in Ijo.

*Zabus*: Is there a stable orthography?

*Okara*: Yes, there is. But there is a shortage of teachers who would be able to teach Ijo in the schools.

*Zabus*: Of course, you cannot train teachers of Ijo, if Ijo is not taught as a medium of instruction.

*Okara*: Yes, teachers have to learn. As an Ijo man, it would be easier for me to learn and to teach Ijo rudiments. I can speak and read Ijo. Recently, Kay Williamson and others have been writing books, readers in various languages in Rivers State, in cooperation with the Ministry of Education. But these books are not yet actually used in the schools, because there is a lack of teachers.

*Zabus*: If Ijo, as you say, is thriving, then it is only orally, through oral transmission, from parents to children. So it is the parent who is the teacher. And what about Ijo art-forms like drama. Are they thriving? Are they popular?

*Okara*: Folklore used to be, but not now. We used to have story-tellers going around villages, telling stories. But not now. In the villages, there are still story telling sessions, but the itinerant story-tellers are no more. The stories still translate Ijo-myths, and they are very much alive.
I tried to put them down in writing, but the manuscripts were destroyed during the war. Now about drama. Years back, during dance sessions, there used to be a break in the dance, when drama

took over. The theme was always about family quarrels, you know, what happened in the family, relationships between man and woman, that sort of stock situation. So, that's the kind of things we used to do.

*Zabus*: What about the myths and legends? Are these still very much alive? Would a teenager know them?

*Okara*: Oh yes. When I go home, I gather the children and I tell stories.

*Zabus*: Who is going to take over from you afterwards? Are there people like you who are natural teachers and natural story-tellers?

*Okara*: Oh yes, there are others who are known as good storytellers of our myths and legends. I have been working on something about Tortoise. Why was Tortoise chosen to play the role of a wise man full of tricks and sometimes treacheries. Why? There are some likely answers. One, Tortoise represents a stage in the developement of the human mind from the primitive or stone age,when might was right or when survival meant the physical destruction of the opponent. Survival of the fittest in physical strength. The Tortoise stage therefore represents the period when Man has settled in farming groups. They had more leisure perhaps to be able to talk about their wars and things like that, as we tell stories in the evening. Before he became a settled farmer, there was a period when might was right. You get what you want if you are strong in the forest. He is settled down now. And he sees that it is not only through might that you can get what you want and that you can also survive through wisdom and mental strength.
Man, shall we say, is a lot like a playwright. He has been thinking of difficult, seemingly insuperable things that could nevertheless be overcome by mental force, not the physical. Now Man thought: "Let's get this little animal to play out all our ideas and let's see." I think they chose Tortoise because Tortoise, as we say, carries his house about with him. Wherever he goes, he goes with his house. He may seem intelligent but he doesn't move fast

108

and could fall prey to bigger and faster animals. So he is in a way weak. Tortoise was therefore invested with intelligence, wisdom and tricks which Man has thought out as weapons to get out of tight situations. Tortoise played his role so well that even Man became one of the victims of his tricks.

Here's an example: There was once a King who had a very beautiful daughter. He gave one condition which a suitor had to fulfil before he, the King,would give away his daughter in marriage. The condition was that the suitor had to remove the King's hair one by one and fit them all back, one by one as they were before. Any suitor who succeeded in doing this would have his lovely daughter's hand in marriage. After all eligible young men had failed, Tortoise said he would also try. So he went to the king with a full cob of corn. He told the King that he was a suitor for his daughter. The King told Tortoise to fulfil the conditions. So Tortoise agreed but he also gave the King the cob of corn and asked him, the King, to remove the grains of corn as he removed his hair. So as Tortoise removed the hairs one by one, the King also removed the grains of corn from the cob, one by one. So in the end when the King said: "Look, you put back the hair" and Tortoise said: "You put back the grains of corn." There was a stalemate. Tortoise faced the King, tricked him, and won.

But time came when Man was satisfied that his ideas had worked out for Tortoise. He was actually testing the relevance, the ability of what he had thought and worked out to be some sort of survival weapons. He reasons with tricks instead of brute force and so when he (Man) was satisfied that he could survive with his tricks, wits and wisdom, he divested Tortoise of all the human attributes he had invested him with. So he returned to assume his natural status as an ordinary animal. Man brought this about in the following way.

One day at the time when people were going to the market, Tortoise also started on his way to the market. Being very slow, he was left far behind. Then he reached a point where his path had been blocked by a fallen tree. So Tortoise stood there the whole morning thinking of how to get over the tree trunk. He stood there until the evening when people who had gone to the market were returning. Tortoise still stood there thinking with his bag of wisdom and tricks over his shoulder. As the sun glowed red and orange, just above the tree tops on its way down the horizon, a boy who was also returning from the market saw him. The boy asked him why he, Tortoise, had been standing there since morning. Tortoise said he had been standing there thinking of a way to get over the tree that had fallen across his path. The small boy looked at the tree trunk and at Tortoise. Couldn't Tortoise have passed through the space between the tree trunk and the ground, the boy said. Tortoise looked and saw what he had failed to see, the whole day standing there. Tortoise stood amazed that it took a little boy just a moment to see what he had to see the whole day. And Tortoise in his annoyance scattered his bag of wisdom all over the world! This is how Man after using Tortoise to try out his ideas of survival without physical force, returned him to his pristine state as an ordinary animal.

*Zabus*: Did you write that down?

*Okara*: Yes. What I would like to do is to do some research to see whether this theme is universal. I already know that there are similar stories of animal wit in other lands. They don't use Tortoise; they use other animals such as Spider and Rabbit or Fox to play the role of Tortoise. What I would like to know is whether in the stories of these other lands the wise and witty animals were also divested of their wisdom and wits at a point, as Tortoise was.

*Zabus*: Do you tell this story to children in English or in Ijo?

*Okara*: In English on television and in Ijo in the village.

*Zabus*: If it was in Ijo, wouldn't that be a good way of teaching Ijo through stories?

*Okara*: Oh yes, of course, but the children in the village all speak Ijo.

*Zabus*: Let us talk about your novel The Voice. Many things have been said about it. What interests me is the future of The Voice.

One would have expected other writers to emulate that kind of style and yet nobody really followed in your steps. How do you explain this?

*Okara*: I don't think that it is quite correct to say that nobody else has tried to write in the way I have done. The thing is they never exactly did, but the idea itself has caught on. The idea, the concept of rendering African concepts, thought patterns, syntax, and other linguistic features through other English devices than calques and loan translations has caught on. I think many people have written and are writing with this concept. But not in the way I have done.

*Zabus*: Do you have anybody in mind?

*Okara*: I brought out the question of this problem in 1962 at the African Writer's Conference in Kampala, Uganda, where I was the first African to talk about this problem. Achebe and others who were in the same conference applauded the idea. It is significant that it was after that conference that Achebe wrote his Arrow of God. This brought him instant fame for his use of Igbo proverbs and axioms informed by the concept I articulated at the Kampala Conference. He may perhaps agree to my statement.
Achebe once said that, "what we are trying to do in a way is an experiment, but if we keep the metropolitan English language, it would certainly have to be able to cope with our experience. In other words, we ought to be able to do something to it so that it can carry our message."[4]

*Zabus*: Do you feel that the Nigerian novel, which is still experimenting with English - Ken Saro-Wiwa is doing exactly that - is eschewing private visions, and moving towards embracing politics like the corruption in Nigeria, talking in less metaphorical terms than you did? They don't use fables or

---

4   Karen L. Morell (ed.) : *In Person: Achebe, Awoonor and Soyinka at the University of Washington*. (Seattle, 1975), p. 27.

allegories. Or do you think novelists are afraid that they may be too direct and then risk being banned?

*Okara*: As you say, writers are now being more courageous, fuelled by their new status in society. It is not just courage alone. It is courage borne out of the feeling of assurance of popular support.

*Zabus*: Then is The Voice courageous?

*Okara*: I think it is also courageous in a way, whether or not it was couched in metaphors.

*Zabus*: Would you have written it in a more direct way today?

*Okara*: Of course, I would have. So what I did was a way of telling the story. The village Amatu represents the whole country; I think that is clear enough.

*Zabus*: But the government didn't feel threatened.

*Okara*: No. They were too busy pocketing their loot to read between the lines of a novel they hardly had heard of.

*Zabus*: So why did you not choose places and characters that exist?

*Okara*: You see, I didn't want the book to degenerate into political pamphleteering. I was thinking of the aesthetic content of the story itself, coupled with the experimentation with the language.

*Zabus*: And would you have considered writing in Pidgin, since that is closer to what is going on in the linguistic arena rather than, say, that kind of artificial experimentation?

*Okara*: I can imagine myself writing in Pidgin. But the problem is that not too many people would be able to read it.

*Zabus*: But Ken Saro-Wiwa writes in Pidgin.

*Okara*: "Rotten English," he calls it.[5] It is not "Pidgin" as it is spoken in Port Harcourt.[6] It has many elements of his own ethnic area, Ogoni, where L stands for R. Thus for Rubber they say Lobber.

*Zabus*: So you wouldn't write in Pidgin because people wouldn't read it?

*Okara*: Yes. For example, Pidgin on the radio is very popular. People listen to it but they wouldn't be able to read it. It is too artificial to be used by writers. It is primarily an oral medium. But if it is written, it is ridiculous. For example, the first poem that was ever written in Nigerian Pidgin was a poem by Frank Imoukhuede, titled "One Man, One Wife". When you read it, it is hilarious. People just laugh.

*Zabus*: So in that respect would you consider writing poetry in Pidgin that would be destined to a Pidgin readership, Pidgin speakers?

*Okara*: No, I haven't thought of anything like that. It does not come naturally to me.

*Zabus*: In the anthology European-Language Writing in Sub-Saharan Africa, there is a chapter on the "older generation" - about you and your contemporary, T.M. Aluko.[7] What do you think of that pairing off? Wouldn't you have liked to be paired off with someone like Achebe, since Aluko is concerned exclusively with chronicles of urban life?

---

5   In his novel Sozaboy. (Ewell, Epsom: Saros International, 1985).
6   A town in South-East Nigeria, where both Okara and Saro-Wiwa live.
7   Patrick Scott: "The older Generation: T.M. Aluko and Gabriel Okara."
    Albert S. Gérard (ed.): *European-Language Writing in Sub-Saharan Africa* (II). (Budapest, 1986), pp. 689-697.

*Okara*: I don't know why I was paired off with T.M. Aluko. I think it was a bad pairing off, myself. What are the criteria? Is it age? It doesn't matter what or how we write? I think the critical delineation of this literary history should be stylistic, or maybe thematic, instead of age. Certainly not the age of the writers.

*Zabus* : So who would you like to be paired off with? As a writer, who is closest to your concerns in Nigeria nowadays?

*Okara* : Almost everybody; almost all writers, young and old, say something about the Nigerian situation, the corruption, for example. I have something coming out early next year, I hope. I wrote a column for a local newspaper, The Nigerian Tide, which I established. I wrote these pieces between 1977 and 1978 as satires of the Nigerian situation between those years leading up to the military coup. The column was on politics and corrupt politicians and degradation of moral values and that sort of thing. It was written in a humorous sort of way, because humour is a way of fighting moral laxity rather than spelling it out explicitly. So, that's being edited now and it will be published in book form.

*Zabus*: Let us conclude. What about this new novel that you have been working at? Do you expect it to take shape? I was told it was about the making of a cynic. People are expecting something, aren't they?

*Okara*: Yes, all I need now is a quiet period, a place for at least six months, something like a writer-in-residence position. And then it would come out. It is about Nigeria; my personal experiences fictionalized. I am the cynic, but not succeeding at that role.

*Obiora Udechukwu*

## QUESTIONS

*I*
*HOW MANY baskets of water can mould a block?*
*How many he-goats can guard a yam barn?*
>*And we talk of yam-masters*
>*But their sons eat* alibo.

*Fish that lives in the ocean*
*That same fish washes with spittle.*
>*And you talk of hell*
>*Does it need death to arrive?*

*The question looms in the evening cloud*
*It hangs so it's now part of the sky*
*The question their chiefs do not want to see*
*The question that questions their stools.*

*II*
*IF THE TEACHER cannot flog the pupil*
*Has he read her book?*
*If the minister cannot rebuke the carpenter,*
*Was he annointed with charmpain?*
*Our feet must go on*
*For their masquerade is abroad.*

*Obiora Udechukwu*

## *TOTEM OF LAMENT*
### *PRELUDE*

*IF MY SCARLET sorrow should impale you*
*Where you walk silent across the field*
*If my purple laughter has faded*
*And the fractured moon, in the aftermath,*
*should stagger*
*If this my voice be muted*
*Before the festival of flutes*
> *Let the song still be sung*
> > *in your heart*
> *Let the song still be sung*
> > *when lights are out*

*For wehn the agonies of a generation are measured*
*And the tree-trunks of the people laid out,*
*Shall there*
> *in the bayonet-fenced field be left*
> *voices to raise a song*
> *for the totem lost in the whirlwind?*

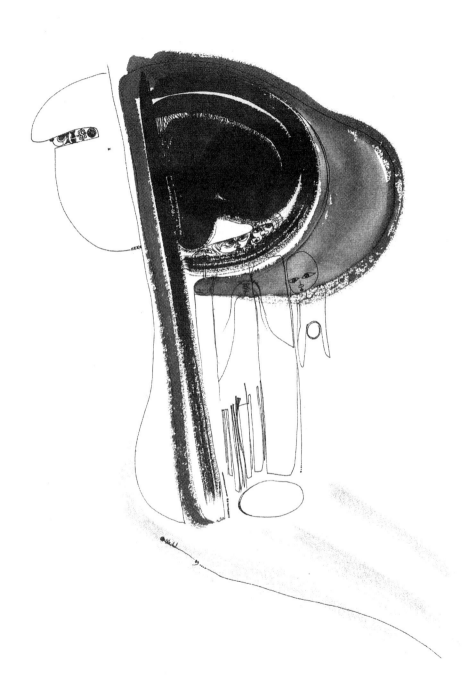

**Obiora Udechukwu**

## *CODA*

*COURAGE, friend*
*Marriage does not kill one*
*Courage, friend*
*Marriage does not eat one.*

*If lizard jumps into the water*
*Should the rat "follow your leader" (one,*
*two)?*
*Do not fish in hurry's water*
*Ijele can disintegrate.*

*And the point?*

*Provided the masquerade arrives*
*Where something happened.*

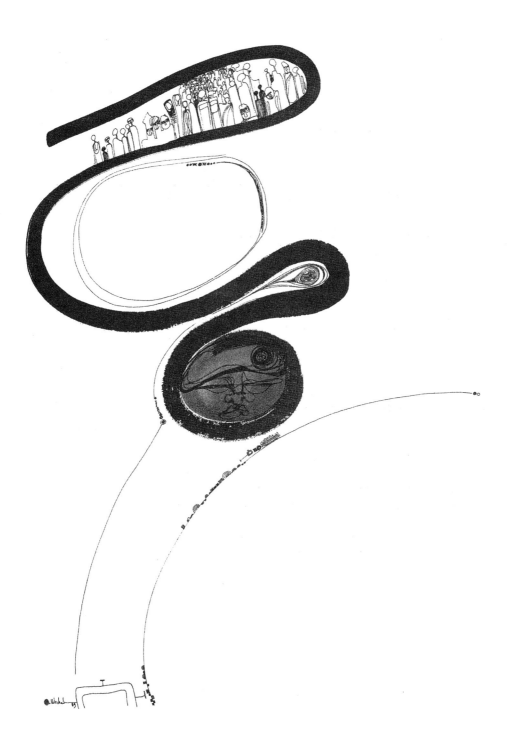

*Taban lo Liyong*

## MRS. VAN RIEBECK TEACHES HER DAUGHTER TO BECOME A BOER

*Stop making circular cakes*
*only Kaffirs make meallie bread that way.*

*Play not in the sand drawing circular*
                                    *huts*
*Ours are rectangular, square, and stoep.*

*Remember to say your prayer at night*
*Our Christian heritage has to keep.*

*Tuck your blouse in, we are Westerners*
*Only Last Indians leave theirs out.*

*Do not eat at the ayah's*
*For their stink comes from their food.*

*Don't cry when a nigger is near.*
*You're the boss even in games and sports.*

*Stop taking my drugs to the niggers*
*The sicker they're the better for your growth*
*And if they died, the better for us all.*

# »Eagle on Iroko«: A Symposium for Chinua Achebe's 60th Birthday. University of Nsukka, Nigeria, February, 12-14, 1990.

During three hectic days in February, Nsukka, the academic centre of Igboland, hosted more than 200 Nigerian and foreign scholars, critics, writers, and diplomats in an excitingly dynamic endeavour to lionize and criticize Chinua Achebe and his works. One must admit that it was the celebration that took over and it did so exultantly.

Most of the 184 papers that had been registered were shortened into cryptic statements, or simply withered away in the Nsukka heat. The 12 sessions that were structured around various themes collapsed helplessly. But at least this gave fruitful leeway for interactions of all kinds and one could see the participants frantically exchanging notes, addresses, and gossip. No doubt, somewhere, Achebe scholarship expanded.

But what about the celebration? The whole of the first day became an odd and dynamic Igbo-English mixture of pomp, cultural events and political manifestations. Breathtakingly bumptious addresses and harangues were delivered, kola nuts were broken, names of present celebrities and dignitaries from both Nigeria and abroad were evoked. The military governor of Anambra State, Colonel R.N. Akonobi, took one and a half hours to arrive, and promptly launched on a scathing attack on the present university lecturers, accusing them of teaching subversive doctrines and supporting "clandestine" student's organizations.

This was followed by hissing and booing; the Nigerian national anthem, Arise O', Compatriots - Zu Oku Nigeria, was sung in Igbo for the first time; and Professor Chinmere Ikoku described Achebe as a "literary luminary, a National Award winner, a social critic, an activist and a patriot". The Nigerian chapter of PEN presented him with a solidarity message; Wole Soyinka - who was not present - sent a white ram; the Ogidi union from Achebe's home town and the governments of Imo and Anambra states donated money for the building of an Achebe library and Research Centre.

In addition there were dramatic performances, such as Emeka Nwabueze's When the Arrow Rebounds, a recreation of Arrow of God; book and art exhibitions by the Ulli Nsukka School; masquerades and poetry readings. Finally, at the banquet, Chinua Achebe gave a speech in which he reminded his audience of the reciprocity and the interdependence of the writer and the readers: The eagle needs the iroko tree.

*Raoul Granqvist (Umeå)*

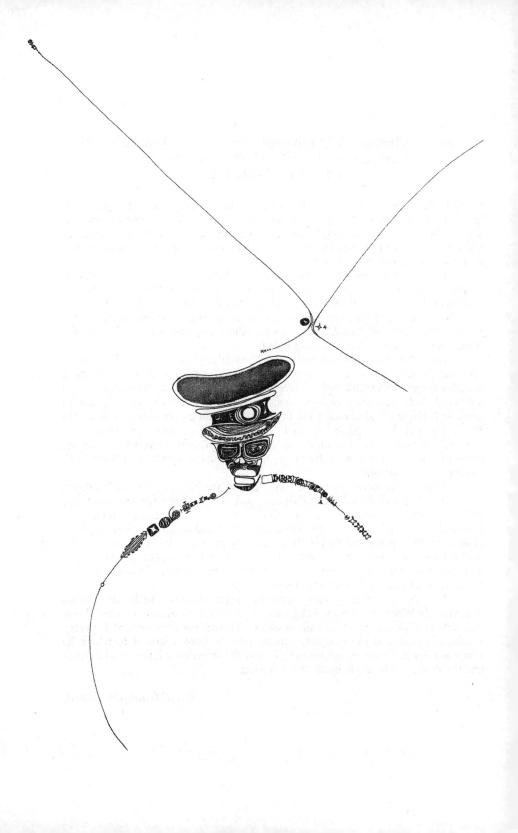

C.L. Innes: *Chinua Achebe*. [Cambridge Studies in African and Caribbean Literature; 1] (Cambridge, New York: Cambridge University Press, 1990). xvii, 199 pp., £ 25.00.

Raoul Granqvist: *Travelling: Chinua Achebe in Scandinavia - Swedish Writers in Africa*. [Umeå Papers in English; 11] (Umeå: Dept. of English, 1990). iv, 76 pp.

Innes' study of Achebe and his work is the first volume in a major new series, launched by prestigious publishers, Cambridge University Press. As the blurb on the backcover tells the reader, the series is designed to

> ... contribute to a wider understanding of the humanistic significance of modern literature from Africa and the Caribbean through the scholarly presentation of the work of major writers.

It is hence not unbecoming for the series to start with a study of Achebe's works, the writer who has established himself as the originator of modern African literatures, showing ways for independence from literary roles and models assigned by European forms and critics.

The book by C.L. Innes lives up to the expectations raised by the self-assigned task of the series. It turns out to be not one more close-reading of the works of the master, as most others seem to be - carefully done, but lacking in originality. Innes's study is precise, innovative and her points are made convincingly. The book is subdivided into nine chapters, with an introduction, a chronology of Achebe's life and a useful bibliography of primary and secondary materials. Although this bibliography is mainly based on the one contained in Innes/Lindfors,[1] it lists all the major studies on Achebe that have been published since then.

In her study, Innes wishes to

> ... place particular emphasis on Achebe's Africanization of the novel, trying to discern what elements he has used and what innovations he has made in his development as a novelist. (p.2)

To her, Achebe's writing has undergone changes inflicted by the experiences of Civil War and the peace-time politics that followed. He alludes to this kind of politics in the title of a story: "Civil Peace" - a society that has adopted the principle of war as a way to deal with everyday life.

Correctly, Innes marks the importance of Achebe's work for his fellow-writers:

... Achebe may be deemed the "father of the African novel in English". [...] His influence is most obviously apparent in the work of younger Igbo novelists such as Nkem Nwankwo, John Munonye, Chukwuemeka Ike, and Flora Nwapa, who follow Achebe in choosing for their settings traditional or changing rural communities, exploring the theme of conflict between old and new values. [...] Achebe's use of "African English", drawing on the proverbs, tales and idiom of a traditional Igbo culture, becomes the norm. (p.19)

The guiding line in Innes's study is Achebe's reaction to "colonial writing", especially the works of Jospeh Conrad and Joyce Cary. Throughout the book, Innes shows how strongly Achebe's wish to create a non-distorted picture of Africa informs his works. Linking Achebe's first novel, *Things Fall Apart* to Joyce Cary's *Mr. Johnson*, she shows the influence the latter had on the creation of the book. Cary's distorted and overtly racist depiction of an African is regarded by her as the driving force that made Achebe become a writer (p.12), in order to provide a "less superficial picture" of African life. (p.21)

Innes shows that *Things Fall Apart* takes up the ideological impetus of Cary's novel, (p.21/22) while *No Longer at Ease* rewrites the story of *Mr. Johnson* itself, introducing a hero - Obi Okonkwo - whose character echoes Johnson's. (p.42) Obi Okonkwo is sent to England to study, returns and joins the civil service. He accepts bribes and is tried for corruption - a fallen hero who served a wrong cause, the cause of the white man, as Johnson has done who goes out of his way to help build a railroad and is finally executed for murder.

Obi Okonkwo is interpreted by Innes as being the embodiment of what Achebe dislikes most: like "The Man" in Ayi Kwei Armah's *The Beautiful Ones Are Not Yet Born*, Obi is "pale, passive", his "pessimism of the west" is his real problem in coming to terms with African society. (p.63).

Even *Arrow of God*, the story of the priest Ezeulu, is convincingly fitted into the intertextual pattern described by Innes. She describes Achebe's third and, perhaps, his best novel, as being "the story of the interaction between colonists and colonized" (p.64). The relation with Cary's *Mr. Johnson* is of a parodistical nature: both Cary's colonial administrator Mr. Rudbeck and Achebe's Mr. Wright undergo strikingly similar situations and experiences, and both are not able to cope with the position they have been assigned. There are also many allusions to Conrad's *Heart of Darkness*, as Innes points out (p.66); thus *Arrow of God*, by constructing these and other parallels, can be seen as Achebe's comment on the novels of Cary and Johnson.

The remaining chapters of the book are devoted to *A Man of the People* and *Anthills of the Savannah*, and his poetry, stories and essays. All of her points are superbly argued and well written. After all, Innes's book is an impressive example of clarity in argumentation. This is shown throughout the text, and her definition of the importance of language in Achebe's work is a fine example:

> For Achebe, the problem of artistic expression and the problem of social change are inextricable [...]. The reader's task is to be aware of the limits of language, to be alert to the ways in which words, formulas and rhetoric can obscure understanding. [...] The concern with the problem of language and the demand that the reader learn to examine language critically take different forms in Achebe's later novels, but remain crucial to all of them. (p.41)

There is only one feature in the book's organization that I find fault with: the notes to the text are neither given on the bottom of a page, nor at the end of each chapter. The reader has to work his way through the whole book to find the extra-chapter devoted to "Notes". This is not only tiresome and inconvenient, but also unscholarly. It has the psychological effect to make the reader ignore notes and refernces - which is a pity and intolerable.

Innes's book is not only new, but innovative. It is a welcome addition to Achebe scholarship and definitely a highlight.

*****

"I have always believed that good fiction can contain more truth than mere fact," says Chinua Achebe in a lecture contained in the little booklet compiled by Raoul Granqvist. (p.13) A lot of facts and some truths can be found in it. As Granqvist points out in his "Introduction", the collection is diverse. It combines accounts of Chinua Achebe's visit to Scandinavia in October 1988 - he had come for the launching of the Danish and Norwegian translations of *Anthills of the Savannah* - with an outline of Swedish travel-writing on Africa. This somewhat odd combination, however, is saved from ridicule by the author's outspoken refusal to insinuate any factual correspondence between the two parts of the book.

Unusual as the combination may seem, both parts have their merits. The first part, which consists of some 56 pages, is devoted to Achebe's visit to Scandinavia. It is divided into five chapters, three of which are transcripts of readings and lectures given by Achebe during his trip. There is also an interview with Achebe by Raoul Granqvist, and a brief article on the reception of *Anthills of the Savannah* in Scandinavian reviews.

In the first chapter, "Achebe Reading" (p.1-10), Chinua Achebe introduces his rendition of parts of *Anthills of the Savannah* with a few comments on the situation of writers in society, pointing out the agenda of the novel as being about

126

... the relationships between the artist and authority. And this
relationship has always been problematic. It has to be, ... if it is not,
then something is wrong. Because there is no way the poet and the
emperor can have the same agenda. (p.2)

Although these sentences seem to be nothing but ideological platitudes,
they do have their political and personal significance. They are also an overt
criticism of Wole Soyinka's collaboration with the present Nigerian military
government of General-President Ibrahim B. Babangida, a role that has been
criticised vehemently by other Nigerian writers as well.

Achebe's lectures are interesting. In "Myth and Power: The Hidden
Power of Igbo Women", he expands on the role of women in society in
general, and on the character of Beatrice, the heroine in *Anthills of the
Savannah* in particular. He describes Beatrice as being the "most important
character in that novel [...] and ... the centre of hope for the future." (p.11)
Achebe doesn't go about the situation of women euphemistically. Quoting an
Igbo-myth of origin, in which the god Chukwu ruled that "men should control
the world because of their kindly disposition" (p.14), he says that:

... in traditional Igbo society the men ... created explanatory
myths and ideologies to keep women out of political power. They went
further to buttress these masculine precepts with stern effective
practices, such as barring the woman from membership of the secret
societies ... which enforced political decisions when necessary. (p.14)

Achebe tries to find a balance between the political power, indubitably
held by man, and the economical power of women, who controlled the market
in traditional society, and do so till today. This economical power resulted in
political power as well, he says. On the whole, Achebe argues, women always
took an active part in society and "were never really dealing alone with issues
pertaining to women, they were dealing with issues pertaining to society."
(p.18) To him, the mythical role of woman as "Supreme Mother" is not just an
idea, but a fact that makes itself felt in everyday life. Women should take an
active part in politics, he says, insinuating that society would benefit from it.

Achebe's arguments are non-committal, well-intended, but of no
consequence to reality. He does not take up the point made by African women
that men never tried to give women a chance to take leading parts in modern
society in general - and in government in particular.

In the second lecture, "The African Writer as Historian and Critic of his
Society", Achebe postulates that writing, in order to be relevant, has to be
based on what goes on in society. He describes his personal cultural heritage as
being a mixture of tradition and colonialism - the latter "a heritage of
denigration". (p.21) He once again attacks Joseph Conrad and Joyce Cary and

complains that white critics fail to see the racism in the writings of these authors, who he accuses of having created a "literature of denigration" that reflects the political phenomenon on an artistic level. (p.22/23).

Following the lectures we find a chapter titled "Achebe Answering Quesions". These questions, asked at four public lectures he gave in Umeå and Stockholm, touch upon familiar ground - topics as diverse as "The Relationship Africa-Europe", "Literature in Africa and in Nigeria", questions of language and literature, traditional Igbo culture and Christopher Okigbo. Achebe's statements are always within the scope of the positions taken by him on numerous occasions and in the essays collected in *The Trouble With Nigeria* and *Hopes and Impediments.*[2]

It is nice to see an editor try .to keep the original wording of lectures - but the result is not always convincing. Stylistic features which add life to a lecture - interjections, repetitions etc. - prove a barrier to fluency when read. So one would have wished that Granqvist had taken the risk to edit Achebe's lectures more than he has done.

But all in all, this booklet is an interesting collection of bits and pieces of Achebe's thoughts. It gives insights into what makes Achebe "tick" - and this is why it is valuable.

*Holger G. Ehling (Frankfurt am Main)*

1    Bernth Lindfors/C.L. Innes (eds.): *Critical Perspectives on Chinua Achebe*. (Washington, DC., 1978).
2    Chinua Achebe: *The Trouble With Nigeria*. (London, 1985). Chinua Achebe: *Hopes and Impediments*. (London, 1988).

**Derek Wright: *Ayi Kwei Armah's Africa: The Sources of his Fiction*. [New Perspectives on African Literatures; 1]. (London: Hans Zell,1989), ixx,+ 333 pp., £ 36, US$ 60.00**

In 1980 Robert Fraser published his slim volume *The Novels of Ayi Kwei Armah*,[1] a book which recorded only an average success in the effort to do justice to both the individual merits of Armah's novels and to place the artistic achievement of the Ghanaian writer in perspective. Fraser's study had further narrowed its usefulness by omitting Armah's short stories, poetry and essays. The appearance of *Ayi Kwei Armah's Africa: The Sources of his Fiction* by Derek Wright ten years later marks a milestone in Armah scholarship and the place of this Australian critic in that venture.

The book, which developed from the author's doctoral thesis, has two parts: section one comprising an introduction, a chapter devoted to the short stories, two on concepts, entitled "Breaking the cycle: the Fanonian vision" and "The Ritual Background to the Novels", respectively; and the last part containing five main chapters, each of which focuses on a novel, and a conclusion that incorporates the essays; a vast chapter of notes, a bibliography and a well-furnished index.

Naturally, such an organization of the work leads a reader to approach the book with interest, expecting that he would find the relevant background information in the introductory chapters that would link with the discussion of literary works in the main body of the book. This anticipation is heightened by Wright's objective which, he states in the preface, is "to situate" Armah's fiction in their "proper ritual, mythological,political and literary contexts", not to engage in another thematic exploration of the novels - a role Wright acknowledges that Fraser has filled. Since Wright intends his book, like Fraser before him, also "to suit the specialized needs of scholars and students of African literature as well as the interests of the general reader" (vii) the expectation that such basic facts be provided is by no means gratuitous.

With the publication of works like Wole Soyinka's *Myth Literature and the African World*[2] it has been shown that a specific African world view exists; but in order for a critic to be able to write informatively on the "Africanness" of any work by an African, such a critic needs to be familiar not only with critical and anthropological writings by Africans and Africanists but more importantly with specific African cultures, for only by so doing can he or she bring out the essential linguistic and cultural information in the work of the specific African writers without resorting to over-simplifications.

Unfortunately, Wright sets out on his mission harbouring residual doubts about the existence of an African world view, hence his equivocation regarding whether or not to enter "the debate about what constitutes "Africanness" and "African" writing". Inspite of expressing the invidious doubts, Wright defines the Africanness of Armah's imagination as

> an elusive quality that reveals itself to a corresponding subtle and probing critical approach, not a shallow property that can be substantiated or refuted by reference to sociological accuracy, setting or narrative realism. (p.7)

When the above claim is placed alongside Wright's tireless effort throughout the book to tie Armah's writing to specifically Akan ritual background, and the style of the early novels to"the hyperbole of the traditional griot", (p.82) we can clearly see the muddle in the book. As numerous scholars, for example, Eustace Palmer and Arthur Gakwandi, have noted it is precisely only with reference to sociological accuracy, setting or narrative realism that we can establish the Africanness of any piece of writing by an African.

Fraser's brief stay in Ghana enabled him to claim familiarity with the traditions of that country, but sadly he did not make much of these. Wright lays no claim to a similar qualification. He draws heavily from the works of anthropologists like Horton, Eliade and Mbiti and from literary critics such as Izevbaye and Anozie but his lack of first-hand knowledge of the specific African roots of Armah's writing is an agonizing source of limitation in his book. And despite his aim to assume "greater familiarity with the texts of the novels than is assumed by Fraser's book" (vii), Wright has ultimately to fall back on close textual analysis. In fact, it is in the close readings of individual works that the merits of Wright's book largely lie.

The chapter on the short stories shows Wright at his critical best - although there is a problem with the organization of the chapters and I would have preferred an arrangement whereby the chapter on the short stories was placed after the present chapters III and IV, and the stories themselves also included in the discussion in the present chapter IV which should be retitled "The Ritual Background to the Fiction" to reflect the links between the stories and the novels, and finally the essays which definitely merit a more elaborate treatment were separated from the concluding chapter. That notwithstanding, the chapter on the short stories, clearly an expanded version of an earlier article,[3] gives summaries of the individual stories and discusses the links with the novels with impressive skill.

Wright is especially compelling where the preoccupation with the manner in which the stories "anticipate some of the themes of the main fiction" (p.16) does not prevent him from noting the laws of composition that govern the works, often independently. Two main shortcomings are noted in the chapter. Firstly when Wright tries to locate influences, as witness the allegation that "The offal kind [is] conceived after the pattern of Victorian England at the peak of its colonial power", he removes Armah's work from its sociological background, whereas closer to him is a story like Achebe's "Vengeful Creditor" that treats a similar theme of maltreatment of househelps, a common practice in Africa. And secondly, there is what may be termed critical shyness, which results when Wright allows his voice to be drowned by established opinion, as shown by his reading of "An African Fable", in the fashion of Izevbaye, as a piece dealing with the question of perception of beauty (reality) as a question of individual vision. The interpretation sweeps aside the central concern of the story to dramatize the betrayal of African independence dream by the greedy elites. Wright is even more dependent on the views of other critics in explicating Fanon's presumed influences on Armah, often without acknowledgement. He trades generalizations, fallacious syllogisms, and frequently plain illogicalities, as when echoing Fraser, he states that

Fanon furnishes Armah's fiction with two key images: the all-pervasive, saturative white monolith, and the doomed cycle [of the oppressed caught up in] a circle of frustration and to enslaved dependence on it (p.43).

And yet, when Wright settles down to the business of actual exposition, it turns out that what he had labelled Armah's borrowing from Fanon is in reality a coincidence of feeling between the two writers and not necessarily influence of one on the other. All this raises the question whether if we say that "the one-sided reality" in Armah's early fiction comes straight from Fanon, we can also say that the Achebe of *A Man of the People* and Okara of *The Voice* who all give a similar picture of post-independence disillusionment in Africa, are equally disciples of Fanon. Clearly, it must be to the socio-political environment in which these writers produce their works that we should turn, for clues about the shaping spirit of their works. This is precisely what Wright is unwilling to do.

A feeling of inept source tracing that one gets away with in the book arises from Wright's inability to depart from well-known views which he too often repeats with no new insights. Wright is weakest in tracing western sources. While Fraser mentions the English romantics Keats and Shelley, and André Schwartz-Bart's *Le Dernier de juste* and Yambo Ouologuem's *Le Devoir de Violence* as writers and books that possibly influenced Armah, Wright vaguely refers to "the French nouveau roman". He then points to Armah's work as a translator in Paris and Algiers to prove his claim that "there are clearly francophone leanings in all his early work which are unusual in an anglophone African author." Were Wright more familiar with work by Abiola Irele and Es'kia Mphahlele, among others, he might realize that the barriers he erects are non-existent, that

> ... when all is said and done, we Africans have since the beginning been thinking the same thoughts and putting them in the same words, whatever colonial flag has been waved over our heads.[4]

The disappointment of Chapter Four, "The Ritual Background to the Novels" (p.51-80), derives from the lack of thoroughness in Wright's research. The material itself is mistitled since there is nothing in there that justifies the use of the words "ritual background". Here Wright misses an opportunity to bring material from outside the novels that could explicate the specific Akan ritual background in the works. Instead, readers are given vague generalizations such as that "the ritual metaphors of the novels hold out respective prospects of purification, sacrificial regeneration and promethean deliverance" (p.52).

Although his close readings remain as usual diligent, the dearth of what are usually termed pejoratively as "extraneous information" or non-literary content in literature by opponents of the sociological approach in criticism, is a serious handicap. Wright fails to meet the very high standard set for this branch of African literary scholarship by Robert Wren.[5] In analysing *The Beautiful Ones Are Not Yet Born* (Chapter V, pp.81-137), Wright produces no actual data to support his claim that "the novel's vividness, concrete immediacy, and very precise kind of integration ... owe more to African oral tradition and ritual symbolism than to the techniques of western allegory" (p.82).

His brief formal judgements are frequently open to question; for example, in adopting the view that the attempt to convey the communal perspective through the communal point of view (chapters 5, 6 and 7) in this novel is defective, Wright reopens an issue that has long been a subject of much heated debate among Armah critics like Larson, Gakwandi, Achebe, Ogungbesan and Lewis Nkosi.[6] Wright's discussions of time concepts in that novel, although very enlightening, are not original observations. E. N. Obiechina long noted the existence of the phenomenon in the African novel.[7]

However, Wright should be commended for being the first critic to document with such convincingness the dual notions of time - "a western chronometric context" and the "less arbitrary, more organic mode of time" (p.86) - by which characters move daily in Armah's first novel. With much clarity, Wright relates the change in the narrative tempo of the novel to changing notions of time, noting the class nature of time consciousness in the novel: While time flies for the rich - the westernized elite - whose lives are governed by time through which they measure their material acquisitions and achievements, as well as their leisure, it grinds to a standstill for the underprivileged who are trapped, as it were, in endless poverty. The man is in the middle, hence he can "pass occasionally and temporarily from one time space to another" (p.90). Its historical dimension is best illustrated by the movement from the tranquil pristine past of Teacher's memory when time seemed motionless, to the post Second World War upheaval which changed time itself into "an agent of irreversible damage and irrecoverable loss, marked by murder, theft, infidelity, and the collapse of the traditional community under the pressures of the new wealth and fashions which the soldiers bring home from the white war" (p.88).

Turning to the exploration of his ritual thesis in the novel, Wright is not equally convincing. His argument that the man's aspiration is to "lift the community out of its moral and material degradation" (p.85) represents a forced attempt to recast Armah's protagonist into his pre-established mould of a ritual carrier, one "who cleanses the community by carrying its sins and subsequent misfortunes into the wilderness" (p.78). This interpretation contradicts Wright's own insights where he tended earlier to show awareness of Armah's depiction of the man in the direction of social realism. Nor is Wright not glossing over Koomson's enormous individualism by regarding him as the symbol of the pollution which the man needs to cleanse to enable the society to regenerate itself.

While *Fragments* does answer well to the ritual thesis, Wright's description of Naana's religious beliefs and of the cycles of the libation, prayer and sacrifice performed by Foli and Korankye do not show anything specifically Akan about those practices. Wright compounds his problem by misinterpreting the novel which he reduces to the crises of Baako, "the been-to [who] returns from America to an Africa that is more western than the West" (p.64). Anyone more familiar with this novel would testify that the issue is not about Ghana being more western than the West - such a condition is hardly obtainable - but rather the chaos that results when a nation accepts corruption as its cultural norm. Even if post-independence corruption has been closely tied to colonialism in Africa, it would be preposterous still to equate corruption squarely with westernization, and Armah has done nothing of the sort.

To many critics, *Two Thousand Seasons* and *The Healers* which take us straight into Armah's African world through the use of myth/epic forms bordering on magic, provide the best basis for an exploration of the distinctive use made by him of African language literatures. *Why Are We So Blest?*, an intermidiary work standing in between the vast experimentation with the idiom of western realism in the first two novels and the oral forms in the last two, is no less of interest for purposes of formalistic analysis.

The chapter on Armah's third novel, entitled "Colonialism as Erotic Ritual: The American World of *Why Are We So Blest?* shows Wright highlight his disappointment at Armah's putting down of all the woes of blacks at the door steps of whites. Wright thus finds Armah guilty of stereotyping his white characters who are presented entirely as agents of destruction, a vision that Wright alleges comes from racialist black American politics of the sixties. Did Wright expect Armah to disregard all the evidence of the evils perpetrated by colonization? Did he want to see a novel in which whites are more positively delineated as bringers of civilization and enlightenment to a benighted African continent? And so, like Fraser before him, Wright's concern with the novelist's ideology, as well as his own prejudice, prevents him from appreciating the high artistry in the novel which James Booth, has described as "the most powerful work of a novelist of genius".[8]

Wright is able to respond with greater sensitivity to *Two Thousand Seasons* and *The Healers*, presumably because in these works "Armah's narrative makes no simple distinction between foreign vice and indigenous virtue" (p.223). His analysis of *Two Thousand Seasons* particularly brings out the oral expressive devices on which Armah's novel relies, with judicious citations from Okpewho, Soyinka and other critics to buttress the points he explores in a lucid, coherent and unlaborious style. By contrast, the chapter on *The Healers* fails to meet the high standard set by the discussion of the earlier novel. Wright resorts to plot summaries that fail to do justice to the complexity of Armah's narrative, and furthermore wastes valuable space correcting Fraser's reading of the novel, when what is needed is an independent reading that could reveal the layered complexities of that novel.

Wright's conclusion of his extensive study, as I have earlier observed, shows serious flaws. Instead of using the occasion to review the results of his findings in such a way that he could take stock of the achievements made, and map out directions for further exploration, Wright prefers to devote the concluding chapter to summarizing Armah's recent essays. The essays are related to the underlying theories of the novels, his alleged borrowings from Fanon etc. all right, but there is no attempt to penetrate the utterances themselves. Wright makes no effort either to hide his unfavourable disposition toward the radical polemics of the essays, an attitude which does not allow for reasoned critical judgment.

Although by no means a complete listing, the bibliography is striking for its broader coverage, especially, of Armah's own works, than has been availabe previously. Only two items that one would have expected to see - an interview Armah granted a Nigerian journalist,[9] and Armah's essay "Battle for the Mind of Africa"[10] - have managed to escape Wright's diligent notice. There is also a curiosity in the omission of an article by Ayo Mamudu which follows Derek Wright's own 1985 essay in the same issue of *Research in African Literatures*.[11] The single error, which occurs in the entry of Sara Chetin's 1984 *Kunapipi*-essay, "Armah's Women", that is said to be a 1974 publication, should also be corrected.

Despite the weaknesses I pointed out, Wright's book is a stimulating study that should open out new horizons of intellectual pursuit. As such it should have a paper-back edition to make it readily affordable to Armah's numerous readers and anyone concerned with African literature.

*O.S. Ogede (Zaria)*

1   (London, 1980).
2   (London, 1976).
3   Derek Wright: "The Early Writings of Ayi Kwei Armah". *Research in African Literatures* 16 (1985), pp.487-513.
4   Abiola Irele: *The African Experience in Literature and Ideology*. (London, 1981), pp.109.
5   *Achebe's World: The Historical and Cultural Context of the Novels*. (Washington D. C., 1980).
6   Wright surprisingly seems not to be aware of Nkosi's *Tasks and Masks*. (Harlow, Essex, 1981).
7   Cf. *Culture, Tradition and Society in the West African Novel*. (Cambridge, 1975).
8   James Booth: "*Why Are We So Blest?* and the Limits of Metaphor". *Journal of Commonwealth Literature* 15.1 (1980), pp.50-64.
9   Dimba Igwe: "Armah's celebration of silence". *Concord* (Lagos) 12 April 1987, pp.11-12.
10  *South*, August 1987, pp.62.
11  "Reflections in a Pool: Armah's Art on Artists and the Arts". *Research in African Literatures* 16 (1985), pp.514-524. Wright cites his own contribution but leaves out Mamudu's piece.

Chinweizu (ed.): *Voices from Twentieth-Century Africa. Griots and Towncriers.* (London: Faber & Faber, 1988). xi, 424 pp., Pb. £ 6.95.

This is the third publication so far within the context of Chinweizu's project of *The Decolonization of African Literature* (1980) and of *Decolonizing the African Mind* (1987).

Appropriately enough, the anthology's programme could be subsumed under the title "The new sprouting horn is not the entire ram" which is the editor's way, in the wake of Achebe's proverbial style, of pinpointing his "anti-Euro-modernistic" grudge.

The main thrust of his argument, stripped of its belligerent lingo, aims at tilting the balance in African literary discourse towards orature, untouched by neither Arabs nor Europeans, towards non-academic Afrocentric popular literature outside the various ivory towers, with the purpose of instructing an unalienated audience in truly African humanities.

Chinweizu arranges what is available in English rendition under eleven thematic sections which are divided into three parts, "The Arena of Public Affairs", "The Local and Intimate Turf" and "Fields of Wonder". A fair amount of prose, some plays, alternate with poems and epigrams. Works by about seventy individual writers have been chosen, which are programmatically mixed with roughly another seventy texts that are attributed to a variety of about forty ethnicities. Problems of translation are dismissed with the remark that contents, worthwhile contents that is, will always come across as the case of the Bible so convincingly demonstrates. The principle of selection has been the reliable documentation of "twentieth century African conversation about the African experience of life" together with the criterion of more or less immediate accessibility ("intelligible works produced by ordinary mortal craftsmen for mortal readers"). The well-worn reasoning is directed against Taban and Soyinka, sides astonishingly enough with Achebe and Senghor, avoids any reference to Ngugi, Mazrui, or Amuta, let alone Ousmane, but mentions Okot p'Bitek, who - together with Achebe and Alioune Diop - figures also in the dedication.

I fear, in the age of computerocracy anyone interested in the humanities, be they African or European or Asian, should be weary of binary oppositions like folktale versus academic literature. Second, though I share some of the misgivings as far as hermetic writing is concerned, I cannot accept a populist neglect of any formal considerations; after all, there is some difference between a poem and a manual. Third, I find the manner in which the "Soyinka bashing" is conducted grossly unfair and stylistically inadequate. Soyinka's shrill treatment here compares unfavourably with Osofisan's elegant wording of his reservations as a fellow playwright. Fourth, I readily admit that we are all of us slightly schizophrenic nowadays, but even so, why go on about Eurocentric this and Eurocentric that and "pandering to blancophilia and negrophobia of Western racism", and then publish in the old colonial metropolis all the same. We in the centre can surely be quite grateful for the effort, but then I thought the anthology had been conceived for "instruction and entertainment" in the periphery. I shudder at what the equivalent of so many Pound Sterling will be in, say, Nigerian Naira.

It is somewhat inconsistent, I fear, to idolize the unsophisticated African reader, to demand the propagation of popular literature, and then discard the financial accessibility of the product. I can only hope for cheap local editions in the future. Otherwise the rural reader (ficticious) will no doubt sadly shake his head and wonder why you abuse the lion first only to rush to his den for food later.

Apart from the antithesis of Africa and Europe, part of Chinweizu's message should be heeded, since there definitely is a Leavite, Scrutonist revival to be constated, all in favour of the elitist concept of literature for the happy few, of the exclusive canonizing concept of not only mainstream but "crest-of-the-wave" literature. What is alarming though is the fact that some of Chinweizu's reasoning all too easily lends itself to the unfortunately rather fashionable denigration of the intellectual, both in Europe and in Africa.

*Peter O. Stummer (Munich)*

**James Gibbs:** *Wole Soyinka.* **[Modern Dramatists] (London: Macmillan, 1988).**

James Gibbs, one of the leading authorities on the life and work of Africa's first Nobel laureate, brings his expertise and years of research on the materials to bear in this monograph on Soyinka's dramatic work. New readers of Gibbs' critical works will find that this contribution is dauntingly erudite and that he has taken great pains to attach importance to considerations which did not occur to other critics of Soyinka's works such as Gerald Moore, Eldred Durosimi-Jones and Oyin Oguba. Gibbs takes what seemed pedantic to these other critics and weaves the materials into a meaningful dialectical paradigm. This is what sets his book apart from his predecessors in the process of understanding the complexities of Soyinka as an imaginative thinker and dramatic theorist.

In this study Gibbs has two aims: the first is to discover sources of influences in Soyinka's works. He uses the writer's Yoruba background, new materials on his early childhood such as his autobiography, Aké, to trace the development of Soyinka's traditional consciousness as a writer. Gibbs also finds sources which influenced Soyinka in the literary culture of Europe and America. Gibbs remarks that

> ... this alerts us to regard Soyinka as self-consciously working in a literary tradition. He is a writer who is convinced of the validity of re-employing existing material. Like European playwrights, from Sophocles to Shakespeare to Brecht, he regards eclecticism as a right, maintaining that it is what an artist does with borrowed material that is important; what or how much he takes is not significant. (p.28)

Gibbs' second aim is to discuss each play Soyinka has written to date, assessing their place in African and modern world theatre. Matters of performance - character creation and staging details - are presented to discuss Soyinka as director, film-maker, critic and teacher.

The discussion of Soyinka's Guerilla theatre works and of his use of other media like records and films to reach a wider audience with his Unlimited Liability Company reveal a new side of Soyinka as a social critic constantly responding to specific social tensions within his immediate surroundings.

This book should be regarded as compulsory reading for all those interested in the works of Soyinka.

*Ahmed Yerima (Zaria)*

Elena Zúbová Bertoncini: *Outline of Swahili Literature.* [NISABA; 17]. (Leiden: E.J. Brill, 1989). 341 pp., Hfl 98.-

Swahili literature has been taught in many universities and schools in- and outside East Africa, and many scholars have paid attention to the development of Swahili literature. Such an interest existed even during pre-colonial times, and for years now there have been attempts to keep a comprehensive record of the history and development of Swahili prose fiction and its analysis. Loooking at all that has been done by other scholars, including articles and mimeographs, *Outline of Swahili Literature* seems to have made a very significant achievement in bringing up a detailed and systematic account of the historical development of Swahili prose fiction and drama.

Bertoncini's study looks at Swahili prose fiction and drama in both its chronological and stylistic development up to 1987. Although the author's main intention was to prove the point that "modern Swahili literature does deserve a place of honour among African writings, and the Western literary critics should at last move towards recognizing its importance" (p.189), the book is far from being a literary criticism of Swahili literature. One of its good qualities is that it elaborately covers all major issues that have been only half-done in other works by other scholars.

In the Introduction Bertoncini provides a brief review of the development of Swahili literature by introducing authors and their literary works. In this bit the author has managed to prove that the origin of Swahili prose does not differ from that of other African literatures and has elaborated this position better than Ohly did in his *Aggressive Prose*. However, special attention to Mbughuni's dissertation would have given this section a clearer perspective, as Mbughuni made a wider study of the oral and written literature.

The author has tried to work on certain themes that recur in Swahili prose fiction and drama. In the Introduction there is a stronger emphasis on prose fiction than on drama and the reader is therefore not well introduced to drama, which is only dealt with in one chapter. If the author had read Mlacha (1987), she would have discovered that it is not true that "the white man is absent from this literature" and that the Introduction needed to be expanded.

The first chapter deals with Swahili prose fiction in precolonial times. It is in this section of the book that Bertoncini covers the development of Swahili prose fiction from its tale form to the novel. The question of how written and oral forms supplemented each other has not been adequately dealt with. Mbughuni has done considerable work on this, and if the author had extended her arguments to Mbughuni's findings, this part might have gained considerably. However, this chapter has elaborated clearly the importance of early collections and the great proximity in plots and style with the Arabic prototypes. One thing worth noting here is that Bertoncini correlates Swahili tales with European tales. It would have been more interesting if one had been made to see the development of such a relationship.One of the oustanding achievements of this chapter is that it gives a clear picture of Swahili prose fiction before independence.

In the second chapter, the author looks at the literary development in the three East African countries (mainland Tanzania, Zanzibar and Kenya) where Swahili is widely spoken. It is interesting to note how she systematically studied contemporary Swahili prose fiction to give a coherent and clear analysis of this fiction. Indeed, because of its comprehensive nature, her book is a good introduction to those interested in Swahili prose fiction, since it covers works which have been written until recent times. Similarly, a general history of the development of drama is presented in the third chapter. One wonders, however, why Bertoncini did not embark on poetry, so as to provide a comprehensive account of the history of Swahili literature.

The book is a precious treasure not only in so far as the contents discussed above are concerned, but also because of the Bibliography and Appendices. The fairly rich Bibliography covers works of literary critics, while

Appendix 1 is mainly a list of contemporary authors of novels, short stories and plays. This section is significant in that it provides a good and quick reference to authors and their works. The works of these authors are then summarized in Appendix 2. The author has thus given the reader a general picture of contemporary works through a very systematic reference that has not been available so far in the field of Swahili literature. This is a book of prime importance to scholars and students of Swahili literature.

*S.A.K. Mlacha (Dar es Salaam)*

**Flora Wild:** *Patterns of Poetry in Zimbabwe.* **(Gweru: Mambo Press, 1988). vii, 152 pp., 10 Zim$**

Im vorkolonialen Zimbabwe existierten vielfältige, häufig von Musik begleitete Formen der Lyrik:

> There were [...] various kinds of poetry for various social occasions, praise poetry for politeness and the recognition of social values; poetry for condolence at times of death and disaster; critical poetry for the safe-guarding and restoration of social values; poetry for entertainment and narrative; poetry for ritual and poetry for children's games [...]; finally there were the boasts uttered to forestall a fight and to protect one's rights, and the didactic poetry to instruct the young.[1]

Diese Beschreibung der traditionellen Lyrik der Shona, etwa 80 Prozent der Bevölkerung des heutigen Zimbabwe, läßt sich mit wenigen Unterschieden auch auf die der Ndebele, der zweitgrößten Ethnie, übertragen.[2]

In den 50er Jahren etablierte sich eine moderne Shona-Lyrik, die sich zunächst an Formen englischer Dichtung orientierte, vermutlich eine Folge des Literaturunterrichts an oft von englischen Missionaren geleiteten Schulen. In diesen Gedichten - und in den gleichzeitig erscheinenden ersten Shona-Romanen - findet sich häufig eine moralisierende Klage über den Verfall traditioneller Lebensweisen, eine Folge der sozioökonomischen Entwicklung (Industrialisierung, Urbanisierung).

Parallel zur Entwicklung eines politischen afrikanischen Nationalismus verbindet sich diese - auch von Missionaren unterstützte - nostalgische Verklärung des Landlebens mit einer positiven Bewertung der vorkolonialen Geschichte. Das bekannteste Beispiel ist Solomon Mutsvairos Roman *Feso* (1956 in Shona veröffentlicht). Das darin enthaltene Gedicht "Mbuya Nehanda Nyakasikana" ist eine Klage über die verzweifelte Lage eines unterdrückten

Landes, eine für zimbabwische Leser leicht auflösbare Allegorie auf das koloniale Rhodesien.[3]

Viele der führenden Politiker der Befreiungsbewegung - z.B. Chidzero, Chitepo, Sithole - traten in den 50er Jahren auch literarisch hervor. Doch verhinderten die restriktive Veröffentlichungspolitik des *Literature Bureau*, einer halbstaatlichen Einrichtung zur Förderung von Literatur in Shona und Ndebele, und die staatliche Zensur die Entwicklung einer explizit antikolonialen Literatur in Shona und Ndebele.

Ebenfalls auf die 50er Jahre gehen die Anfänge einer englischsprachigen Lyrik schwarzer Zimbabwer zurück. Der Einfluß der Missionsschulen zeigt sich in der häufig religiösen Thematik.[4] Die Hinwendung der Shona-Lyrik zu Formen der Oralliteratur in den 60er Jahren wurde in der englischsprachigen Dichtung meist nicht mitvollzogen.

Angeregt von einigen aufgeschlossenen Lehrern und *creative-writing*-Kursen an Missionsschulen suchte die neue Generation schwarzer Lyriker in den 60er und 70er Jahren nach einer eigenen Stimme. Eine schwierige Aufgabe, waren sie doch durch die repressive Kulturpolitik Rhodesiens von der literarischen Entwicklung in Afrika weitgehend abgeschnitten. Der Kontakt zu weißen rhodesischen Lyrikern - meist Epigonen der literarischen Strömungen in England - blieb oberflächlich, doch boten die von liberalen Weißen getragenen Literaturzeitschriften eine der wenigen Veröffentlichungsmöglichkeiten.

Viele der heute bekannten Literaten Zimbabwes - Zimunya, Marechera, Nyamfukudza - opponierten in den 70er Jahren gegen das weiße Minderheitsregime und wurden von der lokalen Universität relegiert. Im Exil, häufig England, setzten sie ihr Studium fort und veröffentlichten in britischen Verlagen.

Mit der Unabhängigkeit Zimbabwes setzte eine Welle von Veröffentlichungen ein. Zhuwarara/Zimunya verzeichnen in ihrer Bibliographie englischsprachiger zimbabwischer Literatur sechs Gedichtbände, von denen nur drei in Zimbabwe erschienen, hingegen für 1980 bis 1985 vierzehn, die sämtliche in Zimbabwe veröffentlicht wurden.[5]

Flora Wild beschränkt sich in ihrem Buch, das neben einem einleitenden Essay Interviews mit sieben Dichtern und ausgewählte Gedichte enthält, auf die englischsprachige Lyrik. Der älteste interviewte Autor ist Charles Mungoshi (geb. 1947), die jüngste - und die einzige Frau - ist Kristina Rungano (geb. 1963). Zwar wurden die meisten heute bekannteren Lyriker aufgenommen - Hove, Marechera, Mungoshi, Zimunya -, doch wäre es vermutlich interessant gewesen, auch Vertreter der älteren Generation - z.B. Zvobgo (geb. 1935) oder Pote (geb. 1939) - und überwiegend in Shona oder Ndebele schreibende Autoren - z.B. Mutsvairo (geb. 1924) oder Sigogo (geb. 1932) - zu Wort kommen zu lassen. Der Anspruch des Titels *Patterns of Poetry in Zimbabwe* wäre so eher eingelöst worden.

Wilds Interviews mit den Autoren machen deren Hintergrund und Ansichten deutlich. Hove und Zimunya verstehen sich - nicht zuletzt wegen ihrer

Erfahrungen im Befreiungskampf - als politisch engagierte Dichter. (Hove: "I am looking at myself as a writer [...] trying to concretize the goals of my people at a particular point in time". (p.40); Zimunya: "[...] poetry should sustain the people's struggle, hopes and aspirations". (p.66)). Dagegen steht die individualistische Konzeption des 1987 verstorbenen Marechera:

"I myself have chosen the private voice, even when I am dealing with a public theme, simply my own idiosyncratic, perhaps irrelevant or anarchistic vision". (p.135)

Irgendwo dazwischen liegt die skeptische Haltung Mungoshis:

"Politics are a lousy game. The idea of freedom for a country is something it must be fought for, but the rest, I leave it to the politicians". (p.80)

Ähnliche Unterschiede werden in den abgedruckten Gedichten deutlich. So findet sich eine - unheroische - Hommage an einen getöteten Guerillakämpfer (Hove "Death of a Soldier", p.46) neben einem eher resignativ-lakonischen Gedicht (Mungoshi "Sitting On The Balcony", p.87) und persönlichen Bekenntnissen (Rungano "Myself", p.110). Die Spannweite der Auseinandersetzung mit dem unabhängigen Zimbabwe reicht von satirischen Gedichten über die "new class of blacks" (Chimedza, p.124; Gedichte: pp.128-130) zur leicht moralisierenden Beschreibung sozialer Fehlentwicklungen (Zimunyas Harare-Gedichte, pp.75-78).

Bemerkenswert sind auch die unterschiedlichen Haltungen zur Sprachenfrage. Während sich Seyaseya (p.94) und Marechera ausschließlich für Englisch entschieden haben, schreibt Hove - neben Zimunya und Mungoshi - sowohl in Englisch wie auch in Shona:

For me an experience expresses itself in its own language. [...] The experience tells me that this would be well captured in Shona and sometimes the experience comes in English, and if I wrote it in Shona it wouldn't be the same. I don't really see much difference in my writing in Shona or English because you are in the two languages battling with emotional experience. But in Shona I can rely on a whole spectrum of traditional forms I grew up in, experimenting with my tradition. (p.39)

Interessant ist auch Mungoshis Verweis auf den - unbewußten - Einfluß der "oral poetry" auf die Form seiner englischsprachigen narrativen Gedichte. (p.79)

In ihrem einleitenden Essay analysiert Wild die Gemeinsamkeiten und Unterschiede der interviewten Dichter und stellt diese in den größeren Zusam-

menhang der Entwicklung der zimbabwischen Literatur. Zwar teilen die Lyriker eine Reihe gemeinsamer Erfahrungen - Befreiungskrieg, Urbanisierung, die
Zeit nach der Unabhängigkeit mit vielen enttäuschten Hoffnungen -, die die
Themen ihrer Gedichte beeinflussen, aber bemerkenswert ist doch eine "great
diversity and disparity in approach, style and in general outlook" (p.25). Die
unterschiedlichen Strömungen in der Lyrik sind ähnlich den verschiedenen An-
sätzen in der englischsprachigen Prosa. Auf der einen Seite finden sich Autoren, die der Entwicklung einer nationalen Identität verpflichtet sind - etwa
Mutsvairo oder Samkange -, auf der anderen "desillusionierte" Autoren wie
Mungoshi, Nyamfukudza und Marechera. Leider werden die Zusammenhänge
zwischen der englischsprachigen Lyrik und der modernen und traditionellen
Dichtung in Shona und Ndebele nicht aufgezeigt, ein Mangel, dem sich die
Autorin allerdings bewußt ist (p.6).

Insgesamt ist das gut produzierte Buch eine gelungene Einführung in die
englischsprachige zimbabwische Lyrik.

*Peter Bräunlein (Bochum)*

1   G. Fortune: "Written Shona Poetry". *Arts Zimbabwe* 2 (1981/82), p.41.
2   Eine kleine Auswahl von englischen Übersetzungen von traditioneller Lyrik der Shona und
    der Ndebele findet sich in: *Mambo Book of Zimbabwean Verse in English*, eds. Colin and O-
    lan Style (Gweru, 1986). Dieser Band ist die umfassendste vorliegende Anthologie
    zimbabwischer Lyrik.
3   Das Original, eine englische Übersetzung und eine knappe Interpretation finden sich in:
    George Kahari: *Aspects of the Shona Novel.* (Gweru, 1986), pp.171-174.
4   T.O. McLoughlin: "Black Writing in English from Zimbabwe". *The Writing of East and
    Central Africa*, ed. G.D. Killam. (London, 1984), p.102.
5   R. Zhuwarara/M. Zimunya: "Zimbabwean Literature in English, 1966 - 85: A Bibliography".
    *Research in African Literatures* 18.3 (1987), pp 340-342.

**Dieter Riemenschneider (ed.):** *Critical Approaches to the New Literatures in
English. A Selection of Papers of the 10th Annual Conference on
"Commonwealth" Literature and Language Studies, Königstein, 11-14 June
1987.* [The New Literatures in English; 1] (Essen: Blaue Eule, 1989) 155
pp., DM 34,-

Die im vorliegenden Band zusammengestellten Aufsätze sind aus Vorträgen
hervorgegangen, die anläßlich der zehnten Konferenz über "Commonwealth
Literature and Language Studies" 1987 in Königstein im Taunus gehalten wurden. Der Herausgeber definiert den Anspruch des Buches vor allem auf die
Notwendigkeit hin, neue Methoden zu einer adäquaten Betrachtung der neuen
englischsprachigen Literaturen zu formulieren und dabei die jeweiligen kultur-

kontextuellen Gegebenheiten in den kritischen Apparat einfließen zu lassen, d. h. die Gefahr ethnozentrisch gefärbter Argumentation zu reduzieren. Zu diesem Zweck werden komparatistische Ansätze vorgeschlagen, die über traditionelle Interessengebiete der Literaturwissenschaft hinausführen. Trotzdem wird die allenthalben beklagte Literaturlastigkeit zuungunsten etwa der Linguistik auch in dieser Publikation noch nicht überwunden. Die Problemlage in den Studien zu den neuen englischsprachigen Literaturen - die Bezeichnung "Commonwealth - Literature" scheint inzwischen überholt zu sein - ist jedoch weitaus komplexer.

In einer Bilanz der Entwicklung der damals noch "Commonwealth-Studies" genannten Teildisziplin beschreibt Gerhard Stilz für die Jahre 1977 bis 1987 festgestellte Schwierigkeiten für eine Etablierung der neuen Literaturen; angefangen mit der Notwendigkeit, neue theoretische Grundlagen zu schaffen bis hin zu der traurigen Tatsache, daß Lehrenden, die sich mit den neuen Literaturen beschäftigten, dies bisweilen eher zu Karrierenachteilen gereicht habe. Dennoch sieht Stilz in der wachsenden Zahl einschlägiger Seminare und Konferenzen durchaus Entwicklungschancen, so auf dem expandierenden Gebiet der Erwachsenenbildung sowie der Medienarbeit. Voraussetzung wäre eine entsprechende Institutionalisierung.

Helen Tiffin weist in ihrem Aufsatz "Post-Colonial Literatures and Counter Discourse" auf die von europäisch-westlichen Diskursen beherrschte Lebenssituation in den ehemaligen Kolonialgebieten hin und beschreibt postkoloniale Kulturen als besonders geartete Hybridformen "involving a dialectical relationship between ontology and epistemology and the impulse to create and recreate independent local identity" (p.32). Entkolonialisierung ist, so Tiffin, unvollständig geblieben und kann in literarischen wie literaturwissenschaftlichen Bemühungen zwar in der Erhaltung sowie Unterstürzung solcher Tendenzen bestehen, die zum einem fortwährend der Dekonstruktion hierarchischer Beschreibungsmuster von Kulturen dienen und gleichzeitig an der Etablierung eines Potentials von Differenzen ohne Hierarchen mitwirken wollen. Tiffins Vorschlag, alle post-kolonialen Literaturen kulturregional verschieden als Kontra-Diskurse zu beschreiben (p.35), damit vor allem einer Eigenkolonialisierung der neuen englischsprachigen Literaturen über die Klammer einer Sprach- und Schicksalsgemeinschaft zu entgehen, wirft jedoch die Frage auf, ob dadurch nicht kulturelle Äußerungen der postkolonialen Regionen auf bloßes Reagieren gegenüber Eurozentrismen reduziert werden könnten.

Was kann an literaturwissenschaftlichen Methoden der in Europa üblichen Theorieüberfrachtung (p.37) entgegengesetzt werden? Tiffins Ansatz stellt eine Kombination dar aus einer Analyse der diskursiven Eigenschaften eines Textes sowie dessen determinierenden Beziehungen mit seiner materiellen Situation im Hinblick auf die Definition seines Grades an Post-Kolonialität. Es soll ein Feld diskursiver Strategien entwickelt werden, das dem Analysierenden

Möglichkeiten an die Hand gibt, übergreifende Strukturen zu thematisieren, welche Beziehungen innerhalb einer Sammlung unterschiedlicher Elemente regeln (p.37).

Die Integration moderner kritischer Diskurse unter Berücksichtigung historisch gewachsener kulturregionaler Spezifika wird auch von Edward Baugh gefordert. Er gibt zu bedenken, daß die scheinbar langsame Entwicklung in der vergleichenden Literaturwissenschaft wohl auf die begrenzten menschlichen Kapazitäten zurückverweist, was vielleicht wiederum ein den Vergleich retardierendes Überdenken alter Positionen hervorrufen mag. Baugh bemängelt aber auch die seiner Meinung nach falschen Versuche neuer englischsprachiger Literaturen, sich den wechselnden Moden westlich-europäischer Literaturtheorie anzupassen und damit der eigenen Marginalisierung Vorschub zu leisten.

Frank Schulze kritisiert in seinem Beitrag den Versuch marxistischer Ansätze, einen neuen Universalismus zu erstellen, dem alle kulturellen Unterschiede geopfert werden sollten. Allerdings führt er dann selbst mit der Übernahme des Begriffes "Weltliteratur als universales Kommunikationssystem" und der "kontemporären Epoche" zumindest universalismusverdächtige Termini in die Diskussion ein. Schulzes Universalismusbegriff wäre jedoch wohl als ein den kulturspezifischen Besonderheiten Rechnung tragender zu verstehen, dem eine komparatistische Methodologie mit der Erforschung der Funktion und des Potentials eines solchen universalen Kommunikationssystems gerecht zu werden versuchen soll.

Bleibt dennoch die Frage nach den Partizipationsmöglichkeiten an einer Weltkommunikation und vor allem nach den sie bestimmenden Herrschaftsstrukturen. Der Marxismus hat aufgrund der 1987 noch nicht absehbaren Veränderungen zur Zeit ohnehin kein hohes Ansehen, doch das muß ihn - etwa in anthropologischen Überlegungen - nicht gänzlich obsolet machen.

Ideologische Blindheit ganz anderer Art prangert Alamgir Hashmi an. Er sieht beispielsweise in Begriffsbildungen auf "Black" - Black Literature, Black English etc. - nur die Festschreibung rassistischer Vorurteile wie sie in europäischen Anthropologien und Sozialwissenschaften gesetzt wurden. Hashmi sieht einen Ausweg - ähnlich wie Tiffin, Baugh und Schulze -in einem veränderten pluralistischen "Menschheitskulturbewußtsein", das sich neuer Diskurse und damit neuer, entkolonialisierter Sprache bedienen muß. Das Studium neuer englischsprachiger Literaturen müsse über vergleichende Ansätze zu allgemeinen Studien führen, für die es Vorbilder in der Geschichte gebe. Hashmi nennt Dr. Johnson, Virginia Woolf und Goethe, deren Literatur- und Kulturauffassung von einer eher kosmopolitischen Gesinnung zeugten. Konzepte von nationalen Literaturen machen, so Hashmi, heute nur noch wenig Sinn. Er wünscht sich einen "Common Reader" für eine neue, interkulturelle, Weltliteratur: "The common reader of this *Weltliteratur* may one day possess a maximum comparative awareness in order to properly, allow of affection, laughter and argument" (p.73).

Er setzt damit die Einlösung von Potentialen voraus, die zwar von einigen Protagonisten - wie dem von ihm genannten Goethe - ansatzweise praktiziert wurde, für deren Durchsetzung aber bislang historische Parallelen fehlen. Die historisch aber um so klarer zu bemerkende Allgegenwart von Ausgrenzungstrategien in Form von latenter wie offener Diskriminierung ethnischer Gruppen zeigt Eva-Maria Kröller am Beispiel der kanadischen Komparatistik, die unter der starken Dominanz des anglo-irischen Bevölkerungsanteils steht und die die Problemlage auf Konflikte zwischen Anglophonie und Frankophonie einengt. Versuche, eine Nationalliteratur zu etablieren haben sich, so Kröller, durch die sprichwörtliche Identitätssuche Kanadas selbst als Fehlkonzeption entlarvt (p.84).

Das der US-amerikanischen "melting pot-Ideologie" gegenüberstehende ethnische und kulturelle Mosaik Kanadas sei nicht in der Lage gewesen, hierarchie-ärmere Unterschiedlichkeiten zu realisieren. Sie möchte systematische Erforschung nationaler Bilder und ethnischen Stereotypisierens über solche Bilder für die kanadische Geschichte betrieben sehen, die sich auf imagologische (Carl Berger) und kultursemiotische (Lotman/Uspenskij) Modelle stützen, um so der - wie sie sagt - axiomatischen Verbindung von Metaphorik und Realität einflußreicher kanadischer Kritik auszuweichen oder sie abzuschaffen. Interdisziplinäre Studien sollten die häufig einseitigen Resultate einzeldisziplinärer Ansätze überprüfen, ohne allerdings neuerliche Kategorisierung in Begriffen von literarischer Brillanz o. ä. zu begünstigen.

Solcher Kritik an traditionellen Konzepten schließt sich Jörg-Peter Schleser an. Er fordert zunächst ebenfalls die Überwindung der ethnozentrischen Holzwege, um sich dann dem von Kröller angeprangerten Bi-Kulturalismus der anglophonen und frankophonen Kanadier in einer Art parallelisierender Komparatistik zu widmen, deren Nutzen für eine Entlarvung von Ethnozentrismen eher fraglich sein dürfte, wenn ihr keine weitgehenden entideologisierten Zugänge zu kulturspezifischen Strukturen inhärent sind, sondern eher eine Samthandschuh-Taktik gegenüber gängigen Diskursen an den Tag legt.

Die explizite Ausformulierung der Bedeutung gemeinsamer post-kolonialer, interkultureller Strukturen, etwa in kulturanthropologischen Termini, könnte hilfreich sein. Dies könnte andere Zugänge zu eher assimilierten Autoren wie Salman Rushdie schaffen. Colin Smith kritisiert dessen "Unbearable Lightness" und seine Art, seinen Status als "product of traditional privileged British education (public school, Cambridge) with affectionate childhood memories of Bombay and current ties with family in Pakistan" auszuschlachten (p.104).

Der linguistische Teil beginnt mit der Feststellung, daß traditionelle deskriptive und präskriptive Konzepte der Soziolinguistik für die multikulturellen anglophonen Gebiete der ehemaligen Kolonien keine adäquaten Mittel bereit halten. Die einzige Möglichkeit, die Manfred Görlach in seinem Beitrag "The Sociolinguistics of English as a World Language" sieht, ist eher auf dem

Gebiet der Pragmatik anzusiedeln. Ähnlich wie seine literaturwissenschaftlichen Kollegen, welche traditionelle Vorstellungen von Nationalliteraturen stark relativieren, diagnostiziert Görlach für das Konzept einer Sprachgemeinschaft in multilingualen Situationen Nutzlosigkeit (p. 120). Die Möglichkeit, Abweichungen von in "Standard English" üblichem Gebrauch oder Nichtgebrauch etwa der Artikel vorherzusagen, sei so gut wie ausgeschlossen. Die karibischen Inseln haben sich dann auch am weitesten linguistischen präskriptiven und dekriptiven Theorien entzogen (p. 122f.).

Görlach fordert seinerseits "... cooperative ventures between African/Asian and European/American colleagues in interdisciplinary teams", die dann stärker literarische Werke in ihre Arbeit aufnehmen sollten, einer Soziolinguistik des Lesens diejenige der Literatur(en) zur Seite stellen und zum Beispiel fragen, welche Unterschiede zwischen literarischen Werken festzustellen sind, die für den jeweils heimischen und solchen, die für den Weltmarkt geschrieben wurden.

Alles das auf der Basis der Anerkennung des Multilingualismus als dem "normal state of affairs in much of the world", was einer Absage an bisweilen noch anzutreffenden linguistischen Purismus gleichkommt (p. 127). Das pragmatischer gedachte Akzeptieren des Englischen scheint wichtiger als die Erstellung von Grammatiktheorien, obwohl die englische Sprache durchaus nicht überall als "neutral tool" angesehen wird.

Insgesamt weist der Band auf eine sich verändernde anglistische Landschaft hin, die sich neuen - vielleicht in Begriffen von Interkulturalität zu fassenden - Problemstrukturen stellen und entsprechende methodologische Neuorientierungen anstreben müssen wird, wobei es sicherlich noch manche, gerade instituionell bedingte, Hürde zu nehmen gelten dürfte.

*Bernd Schulte (Siegen)*

**Suzanne Romaine:** *Pidgin and Creole Languages.* **[Longman Linguistics Library] (London, New York 1988, xi, 373 p., £ 9,95.**

Es scheint Teil der Marketingstrategie vieler Verlage und Herausgeber zu sein, auch Bücher, die es auf Grund ihrer inhaltlichen Qualitäten nicht nötig hätten, mit Titeln zu versehen, die mehr versprechen als sie halten. Ein Titel wie "English Based Pidgin and Creole Languages" wäre ehrlicher gewesen, zumal die Verfasserin selbst im Vorwort schreibt "... inevitably I have stuck close to the languages I know best in illustrating basic points". Zu diesen Sprachen gehören vor allem Tok Pisin - das Pidgin-Englisch Papua Neu Guineas - Hawaii

Pidgin und Kreol-Englisch, die Romaine durch Forschungs- und Lehraufenthalte aus eigener Anschauung und "Anhörung" kennt.

So kommen französisch-, niederländisch- und deutschbasierte Pidgin- und Kreolsprachen in diesem Buch generell zu kurz, was seine Verdienste aber nur insofern beeinträchtigt, als Daten und Phänomene aus diesen Sprachen manche der einseitig am Englischen ausgerichteten Theorien und Erklärungsversuche relativieren würden[1] (cf. Stolz 1987). Für den Bereich der englischbasierten Pidgins und Kreols als solcher ist, was die Fülle und Vielfalt des dargebotenen konkreten Sprachmaterials sowie die kritische Diskussion der Forschungsliteratur betrifft, Romaines Arbeit vergleichbaren Werken, wie etwa Hellinger,[2] eindeutig überlegen.

Das Buch gliedert sich in Vorwort, acht Kapitel, einen Anhang, der mehr als einhundert Pidgins und Kreols auflistet und z. T. kommentiert, eine umfangreiche Bibliographie, sowie einen Index der Begriffe und Namen.

In der "Introduction to the Study of Pidgins and Creoles" (p.1-22) skizziert Romaine zunächst die Geschichte der Kreolistik seit den 80er Jahren des vorigen Jahrhunderts, diskutiert eine Reihe von Etymologien des Wortes "pidgin" und wendet sich gegen die populäre, aber unhaltbare Auffassung, Pidgins seien korrumpierte Versionen der jeweiligen Superstrat-Sprache (p.13). Sie stellt anhand einer Weltkarte die Verteilung dieser Sprachen dar und vergleicht ihre eigenen Ziele und Absichten mit denen anderer, neuerer Arbeiten, vor allem hinsichtlich der Berücksichtigung von Ergebnissen der Spracherwerbs-, Sprachwandel- und Universalienforschung.

Kapitel zwei, "Definitions and Characteristics of Pidgin and Creoles" (p.23-70) stellt im einzelnen die linguistischen Eigentümlichkeiten von Pidgins und Kreols vor. Die Typen von formalen Vereinfachungen gegenüber den Codes der Superstratsprachen, die in Pidgins auftreten, resultieren nicht notwendiger in Bedeutungsverarmung oder Mangel an sprachlicher Ausdrucksfähigkeit, sondern oftmals in deren grösserer Regularität. Sie können daher als grammatische Sprachen bezeichnet werden, die im Gegensatz zu "lexikalischen" Sprachen wesentlich weniger Primärwörter haben, dieses Defizit aber durch "periphrastische" Konstruktionen und Umschreibungen wettmachen.[3]

Romaine diskutiert auch Kriterien zur Abgrenzung von Pidgins und Kreols. Beide sind reduzierte Mischsprachen mit de facto-Normen, denen in mehr oder weniger starkem Maße Standardisierung, Historizität und Autonomie fehlen. Bei Kreolsprachen gibt es jedoch grössere Gemeinschaften von "native speakers", von Sprechern, die den entsprechenden Code als Muttersprache erlernt haben. In der Forschung ist deshalb auch die Position vertreten worden, daß die Veränderungen, die sich feststellen lassen, wenn Kinder eine Pidginsprache als Primärsprache lernen - sie kreolisieren -, Rückschlüsse auf die wenigstens erforderliche strukturelle Grundausstattung natürlicher Sprachen d.h. deren kognitiv notwendige Minimalstrukturierung erlauben (p.68). Dazu scheinen ca. zwölf linguistische Strukturierungsmerkmale zu gehören, darunter ein Tempus und/oder Aspektsystem, Negation, Frage- und Komplementsätze, Relativisierungs- und Possessivkonstruktionen.

In Kapitel 3 untersucht Romaine Theorien zu "The Origin of Pidgins" (p.71-114). Deren reduzierte Strukturen wurden erklärt als Resultat der mangelhaften Erlernung der betreffenden Standardsprache durch die Sklaven - "baby talk" - oder der bewußten Vereinfachung wie beim "foreigner talk", als Weiterentwicklungen eines "nautical jargon", wie er auf Schiffen von Seeleuten verschiedener Nationalitäten benutzt wurde. Es ist auch möglich, daß relexifizierte Ableitungen aus einem einzigen portugiesischen Kreol, das im 15. Jahrhundert an der afrikanischen Küste gesprochen wurde und seinerseits mit Sabir, der lingua franca des Mittelmeers, verwandt war, zur Herausbildung des Pidgin geführt haben ("monogenetic/relexification-Theorie") (p.86-91).

Auch polygenetische und Substrat-Theorien werden vertreten. Sie nehmen entweder voneinander unabhängige Entwicklungen ähnlichen linguistischen Materials oder ein gemeinsames westafrikanisches Substrat an. Die Lehre, die Romaine aus der Diskussion der Ursprungstheorien zieht, besagt, daß oberflächliche Ähnlichkeiten der Form von Sprachen keine unbedingte Gewähr für einen gemeinsamen Ursprung bieten, genausowenig wie strukturelle Gemeinsamkeit mit Identität der Funktion gleichgesetzt werden kann (p.108).

In vielen Fällen ist eine Erklärung mit Bezug auf linguistische Universalien genausogut möglich. In Kapitel 4 und 5 beschäftigt sich Romaine mit "The Life-Cycle of Pidgins" bzw. "of Creoles". Die Idee, bei diesen Sprachen im Gegensatz zu "normalen"Sprachen von Lebenszyklen zu sprechen, findet sich in neuerer Zeit zuerst bei Hall[4] und ist besonders von Mühlhäusler[5] (1979) verfeinert worden, der innerhalb des Pidgin-Kreol-Entwicklungskontinuums die Phasen "jargon", "stable pidgin", "extended pidgin" und "creole" unterscheidet, die jeweils mit Restrukturierungsprozessen verbunden sein können.

"Jargons" als Verständigungsmittel für sehr beschränkte Kommunikationszwecke sind durch grosse individuelle Variationsbreite, ein einfaches Lautsystem, Ein- oder Zweiwortsätze und ein sehr geringes Vokabular gekennzeichnet. "Stable pidgins" wie z B. Russenorsk, das von russischen Händlern und norwegischen Fischern verwendet wurde (p.124) und auf dessen reduzierte morphologische Struktur und Entstehung Romaine etwas genauer eingeht, haben einfache und komplexe Sätze und, was noch wichtiger ist, gewisse Normen der linguistischen Korrektheit (p.124).

In "extended/expanded pidgins" ist das referentielle und expressive Sprachpotential wesentlich grösser, die Grammatik ist komplex, eine Wortbildungskomponente entsteht und Schnellsprechformen bilden sich aus. Das letztere hat z. B. in Tok Pisin zur Folge, daß es für das frühere, futurische Satzad-

verbial "baimbai" ("by and by") auf seinem Weg zum verbalen Präfix die pho-
nologisch reduzierten Formen "babai", "bai" oder "ba" gibt (p.138).

Hier, wie durchgängig im ganzen Buch, breitet Romaine eine Fülle von
interessanten und z. T. linguistisch überraschenden Daten und Analysen des
Tok Pisin aus. Etwa die Entwicklung der ursprünglichen Präposition "long"
zum verbabhängigen "complementizer" (p.141/142) oder die Grammatikalisie-
rung von "orait" ("alright") als "sentence connective" (p.146-150). Da
Kreolisierung in jeder Phase des Entwicklungskontinuums eintreten kann, sind
die strukturellen Unterschiede zwischen einem erweiterten Pidgin und einem
beginnenden Kreol fliessend.

Ähnliches gilt für mögliche weitere Stadien des Kontinuums, wie die
Entwicklung zu einer normalen Sprache oder die Entkreolisierung im Kontakt
mit einer Standardsprache. So entsteht ein linguistisches Kontinuum von
Kreolvarietäten, die vom Basilekt über Mesolekte bis zum Akrolekt, d. h. der
Standardvarietät, reichen.[6]

Die verschiedenen Probleme, vor die sich gängige systemlinguistische
Modelle mit ihren Homogenitätsannahmen durch solche Kontinua gestellt sehen, werden von Romaine anschaulich dargestellt und diskutiert, einschließlich
des Phänomens der Rekreolisierung, d. h. der zunehmenden, bewußten Verwendung kreolischer Formen als Ausdruck sozialen Protests und persönlicher
Identitätsfindung, wie im Falle des "London Jamaican Creole" (p.188-197).

Kapitel 6 (p.205-255) befaßt sich mit der Pidgin- und Kreolproblematik
aus der Sicht der neueren, theoretisch orientierten Spracherwerbsforschung.
Dabei erörtert Romaine die wichtigsten für Erst- und Zweitsprachenerwerb
entwickelten Erklärungshypothesen und deren Übertragbarkeit auf Pidginisie-
rungs- und Kreolisierungprozesse, sowie die Möglichkeit, solche Prozesse zur
Falsifizierung oder Validierung von Hypothesen heranzuziehen. So ist zwischen Anhängern der kontrastiven Hypothese einerseits und universaler Prinzipien des Spracherwerbs andererseits strittig, ob Lernerfehler beim L2-Erwerb
interferenz-oder entwicklungsbedingt auftreten. Trifft das letztere zu, kann dies
als Bestätigung der sog. "L1 = L2- Hypothese" und der Chomskyschen Theo-
rie der Universalgrammatik interpretiert werden.[7]

Kapitel 7 "Language Universals and Pidgins and Creoles" (p.256-310)
enthält fast ausschließlich Romaines Auseinandersetzung mit Bickertons Bioprogrammhypothese,[8] gemäß der das linguistische Bioprogramm des Menschen
vier semantische Unterscheidungen enthält: 1. spezifisch/nichtspezifisch; 2.
Zustand/Vorgang; 3. punktuell/nicht punktuell und 4 kausativ/nicht-kausativ.
Danach ist eine Kreolsprache als die Realisierung der Instruktionen des Biopro-
gramms mit minimalen kulturellen Beimischungen zu definieren.

Im Verlauf der Diskussion der unterschiedlichen morphosyntaktischen
Realisierungen dieser semantischen Unterscheidungen in verschiedenen Spra-
chen und deren Varietäten kommt Romaine auf eine der methodologischen
Hauptschwächen der linguistischen Universalien- und der Spracher-

werbs‼forschung zu sprechen, die Überprüfbarkeit der jeweiligen Hypothesen. Wenn die Teiltheorien und Prinzipien der syntaxorientierten Chomskyschen Universalgrammatik auf Grund ihrer Parametrisierbarkeit nicht mehr falsifizierbar sind[9] und zwei Untersuchungen derselben Kreoldaten zur Bioprogrammhypothese entgegengesetzte Ergebnisse zeigen, weil die durch die Sprecher "beabsichtigten Bedeutungen" anders interpretierbar sind, ist das für die Plausibilität und Glaubwürdigkeit der in Frage stehenden Thorien genauso verheerend, wie wenn man glaubt, aus den Reaktionen und Produktionen von Kindern auf diese oder jene universelle Erwerbssequenz von Tempora, Aspekten und Modalitäten schliessen zu können, obwohl deren Effekte in Abhängigkeit von der Aktionsart der jeweiligen Verben sogar bei erwachsenen Sprechern schwer zu bestimmen sind (p.283).

Darüber hinaus ist nicht auszuschliessen, daß der Erwerb bestimmter Strukturen durch soziale Faktoren, z.B. geschlechtsspezifische Verwendung, verzögert wird (p.289) oder sogar, daß sozial überlieferte Charakteristika einer Sprache, ihre kulturelle Entwicklung, die biologischen Universalien im Einzelfall überlagern können (p.309).

In Kapitel 8 "Conclusion" (p.311-314) weist Romaine als Fazit vor allem auf zwei Faktoren hin, die weitere Fortschritte in der Kreolistik behindern: zum einen das Fehlen adäquater Modelle und Theorien des Sprachwandels und der "Entwicklung" und zum andern die Forschungsdefizite hinsichtlich der sozio-historischen und sozio-linguistischen Voraussetzungen von Pidginisierungs- und Kreolisierungsprozessen. Ihre eigene Arbeit sieht sie als Versuch, für eine entwicklungsorientierte Sprachtheorie zu argumentieren, die alle Erwerbsphänomene in ein einziges Modell inkorporiert.

Dieser Versuch ist, so meine ich, weitgehend gelungen. Einige Kritikpunkte sollen abschliessend noch genannt werden: Da z.B. Phrasenstrukturregeln im Format der Chomskyschen "X-bar"-Theorie (p.47, p.141) nicht unbedingt zum "elementary knowledge of linguistics" (viii) gehören, sollte die zweite Auflage um ein Glossar linguistischer Begriffe erweitert werden. Als Leser würde man auch gerne erfahren, daß Unserdeutsch, das im Index mit zwei Verweisen auftaucht, auch Rabaul Kreol genannt wird und ein aussterbendes deutschbasiertes Kreol ist, das in Papua Neu Guinea und in Queensland, Australien, noch vereinzelt gesprochen wird.[10]

*Hans Ulrich Boas (Göttingen).*

1 T. Stolz: "Kreolistik und Germanistik: Niederländisch-basierte Sprachformen in Übersee". *Linguistische Berichte* 110 (1987), 283-318.
2 Marlies Hellinger: *Englisch-orientierte Pidgin- und Kreolsprachen.* (Darmstadt, 1985).
3 Vgl. z. B. Tok Pisin "singsing long taim maus i pas" ("mit geschlossenem Mund lange singen = summen") oder "gras bilong fes" ("Gras des Gesichts = Bart") und "gras bilong hed" ("Gras des Kopfes = Haare") (35). Statt der willkürlichen Zeichen "hum" oder "beard" und "hair" in der lexikalischen Sprache Englisch stehen also im Tok Pisin motivierte Zeichenkombinationen.

150

4 R.A. Hall: "The Life-Cycle of Pidgin Languages. Festschrift De Groot." *Lingua* 11 (1962), 151-156.
5 Peter Mühlhäusler: *Growth and Structure of the Lexicon of New Guinea Pidgin* [Pacific Linguistics; C-52], (Canberra, 1979).
6 Vgl. z. B. die Situation auf Jamaica.
7 Cf. Hans Ulrich Boas: *Formal versus Explanatory Generalizations in Generative Transformational Grammar* (Tübingen, 1984).
8 Derek Bickerton: *Roots of Language*. (Ann Arbor, 1981).
9 Cf. Hans Ulrich Boas: "Parametrization in Generative Grammar". *Anglistentag 1987 Tübingen. Vorträge*, ed. H.W. Ludwig. (Giessen, 1988), 406-409.
10 *Ethnologue, Languages of the World*, ed. B.F. Grimes. (Dallas, Texas, 11th ed., 1988).

*Imperialism and Popular Culture*, ed. John M. MacKenzie. [Studies in Imperialism]. (Manchester: Manchester University Press, 1986), vii, 264 pp., £ 10.95.

Students of culture have begun to understand that the distinctions between highbrow, middlebrow, and lowbrow culture are futile concepts. Even leftist culturalists like Donald Lazare claim that revisions have to be made as

> ... high art has increasingly incorporated popular culture and vice versa, often with vitalizing effects for both. Middle America has discovered Baryshnikov and Brie, while intellectuals praise "Hill Street Blues" and Larry Bird".[1]

Cultural productions travel across the economic and political boundaries leaving imprints of their unquenchable urge for intermarriage between oral culture and print culture, between folk culture and mass culture - again, whether we approve of it or not. In most cases, however, these marriages have been scorned as bastard and illegitimate. As a matter of fact, cultural analysts have far too long nurtured a romance for whatever could be defined as "folk" or "oral", without accounting for the overpowering complexity that informs the cultural expression. This is not to say that the Marxist or socialist point of view and method in cultural analysis are outmoded and should be ignored. On the contrary! In a mass media world that is becoming so intricate and so powerful, where manipulation and repressive tolerance are the hallmarks of most capitalist domination, they are more than ever required as tools to explicate the cultural reflections of class and power and of race and sex. It is just that an older dogmatist or sectarian view-point camouflages and distorts the progress towards the "truth" or, as we would prefer to phrase it today, the "truths".

*Imperialism and Popular Culture* seems to bear out the validity of the above remarks. In his cogent introduction to the anthology, John M. Mackenzie, lecturer in history at the University of Lancaster, makes two significant concurrent declarations. Historians, he claims, have been concerned with the offical image of imperialism, with its political, strategic and economic dimensions, but not in terms equal with its psychology, with its popular aspect. Thus they have not seen that the national elite (British in this case) promoted imperialism through the creation of new rituals and cults, i.e. such as the inter-war Empire Day concerts and the Scout movement, which in fact were part of systems inherent in existing popular traditions. "It might indeed be argued", says MacKenzie, "that the truly popular culture is one which crosses class lines, ... whether that cross-class- interest was engineered from above or demanded from below is, of course, another matter (p.9)". The convergence of pursuits, national and popular, is then what underpins the effectiveness of national propaganda. A study of the mechanisms and impacts of popular culture within any historical or thematic reference must therefore admit of a broad integrative approach. This is one of the major assumptions posited by MacKenzie's book.

MacKenzie's contention is that imperial nationalism, through its semblance of creating unity across class and culture, was influential long after it had lost its *imperialist* aggressiveness at the time of the Boer war. By being *imperial* - retention of an existing superior Empire, rather than acquisition of new provinces - it had penetrated into the soul of the people, many of whom might even declare themselves anti-colonial. This inevitably leads to MacKenzie's second overriding view that historians of imperialism and of popular culture necessarily must work together. He offers this volume as a preliminary attempt at achieving the propagation of this conjecture.

So far I have dwelt on aspects of his book that are of theoretical interest for any cultural critic engaged in the current debate on third world cultural dialectics. Let me be more concrete. In the mould of nine well-researched essays, the book surveys the interaction of British imperialism and media activities between the late nineteenth century and the beginning of World War II. With four essays dealing with subject matters related to the pre-Great War period and four to the inter-war years (with the fifth right in the middle), the organization of the book assists in demonstrating that the imperial state of Great Britain was a continuous affair that did not stop, as commonly believed, with victory in war. Certainly the "victory" over Argentina in the Falkland Islands soap opera skirmish seems to call for further courageous research into the institution of popular culture and imperialism in the British post-Second World War era.

The topics treated are multifarious, ranging from examinations of Victorian jingoist patriotic spectacles and "blood and thunder" melodramas (Penny Summerfield), to discussions of imperial iconography of the heroic (John O. Springhall), juvenile, racist fiction of historical romances (J.S. Bratton), showbiz imperialism, featuring the African Peter Lobengula and his Matabele troup (Ben Shephard), inventions and the propagation of new national rituals by, for example, the BBC and the Empire Marketing Board (J.A. Mangan, Stephen Constantine, John M. MacKenzie), the making of adventure films, such as Michael Balcon's *Rhodes of Africa* steeped in the militarist ethos of the public school (Jeffrey Richards), and the fake internationalism of the Scout movement (Allen Warren). This last essay is the only one that I find disappointing: it suffers from reverence for the subject it is treating. Baden-Powell's bigotry and eurocentrism is not sufficiently accounted for. Furthermore, many of the essays lack perception of the rôle race played (and still plays, although differently) in British imperial expansion.[2]

If anything, MacKenzie's book makes it perfectly clear that the "energising myth of the Empire"[3] needed collaborators in all fields of culture and politics to materialize. It comes therefore as no surprise that fiction, music-hall entertainment, film, painting etc. were basically filtered through the same metaphors and projected the same protagonists. The most frequent protagonist is the imperial civil servant (the soldier, the sailor, the Scout) fighting for the English version of freedom (which also typifies the "white man's burden") and the key symbol that evokes and inspires his mission is the allusion to a homely St. George, the heroic red-cross knight, who combines chivalrous conduct and consideration for others with aristomilitary aggressiveness. The killing of the dragon is, then, a telling metaphor for the subjugation of the Other, i.e. imperialism and popular culture walking and working hand in hand.

I find MacKenzie's book both challenging and innovating in its broadening of the assumptions regulating the interplay of culture and power. And even more so because it leaves so many questions unanswered, some of which MacKenzie poses himself. "How successful were popular cultural vehicles in conveying an imperial world view to the British public? Were popular ideas merely a reflection of, or were they instrumental in imperial policy? (p.10)". And one could add others: To what extent, and how, was British imperialism reflected or underpinned by other European countries? What connections were there between British and, say, French or German imperialism and popular culture during the "scramble for Africa"? And many others.

*Raoul Granqvist (Umeå)*

1   Donald Lazare (ed.): *American Media and Mass Culture: Left Perspectives*, (Berkeley, Los Angeles, London, 1988), pp.2.
2   Charles Husband (ed.): *"Race" in Britain: Continuity and Change*. (London, 1985).
3   Martin Green: *Dreams of Adventure, Deeds of Empire*. (London, 1980), pp.20.

Iain Christie: *Samora Machel. A Biography.* (London: Zed, 1989). 181 pp., Hb. £ 26.95; Pb. £ 7.95.

The name Samora Machel stands for many things. Not only was he an extraordinary leader of his country - until his sudden death in a plane crash on October 20, 1986; his name is also representative for the history of Mozambique and its struggle for liberation.

Born 1933 in what is now the Chokwe District of Gaza Province, the third child of a farmer who had worked in South Africa was luckier than other children. His father was prosperous and could afford to send his son to school. Machel's rebellious spirit was roused during his training as a male nurse, when he came to know the system of forced labour, repression of national consciousness and the institutionalized humiliation of Africans.

These issues and his encounter with the nationalist leader, Eduardo Chivambo Mondlane, inspired him to join FRELIMO (Frente de Libertaçao de Moçambique), which had been founded in 1962 in Dar es Salaam. "He was at war for the last 22 years of his life; fighting for the peace of his people" says Christie in his biography. While the Portuguese imperialist régime received increasing economic and military support from western nations, Machel strengthened FRELIMO's ties with sympathizers in socialist countries, finally achieving his goal in the independence and the establishment of the Republic of Mozambique.

Iain Christie's biography of Samora Machel not only describes the history and development of FRELIMO from its birth to 1986, the author also draws a compelling portrait of its leaders, especially of Samora Machel, who was to become president of independent Mozambique. Christie, who joined FRELIMO in 1970, was able to obtain a close view of Machel, whom he describes as an impressive politician and a charismatic personality. Thus it is understandable that Machel has, since his death, become a martyr in his country.

Christie does not conceal his sympathy for Machel, the person and politician. Although the book lacks criticism of Machel's ideology, it is well worth reading for anyone interested in the political history of southern Africa.

*Andrea Schlosshan (Frankfurt am Main)*

154

Author's Addresses - Adresses des auteurs

Patricia Alden, English Dept., St. Lawrence University, Canton, NY 13617, USA

Hans Ulrich Boas, Seminar für Englische Philologie, Universität Göttingen, Humboldtallee 13, 3400 Göttingen, GERMANY

Peter Bräunlein, Dorstener Straße 1, 4630 Bochum 1, GERMANY

David A. Maughan Brown, Dept. of English, University of Natal, P.O. Box 375, Pietermaritzburg 3200, SOUTH AFRICA

Holger G. Ehling, In der Au 33, 6000 Frankfurt a.M. 90, GERMANY

Ezenwa-Ohaeto, Dept. of English Language and Literature, Anambra State College of Education, P.M.B. 5011, Awka, Anambra State, NIGERIA

Marlies Glaser, Institut für England- und Amerikastudien, Johann-Wolfgang-Goethe-Universität, Kettenhofweg 135, 6000 Frankfurt a.M. 11, GERMANY

Raoul Granqvist, Dept. of English, University of Umeå, 90817 Umeå, SWEDEN

S.A.K. Mlacha, Institute for Kiswahili Research, University of Dar es Salaam, Dar es Salaam, TANZANIA

Chimalum Nwankwo, Dept. of English, College of Humanities and Social Sciences, North Carolina State University, Box 8105, Raleigh NC 27695-8105, USA

O.S. Ogede, Dept. of English, Ahmadu Bello University, Zaria, NIGERIA

Tayo Olafioye, Dept. of Modern European Languages, University of Ilorin, PMB 1515, Ilorin, NIGERIA

Bode Osanyin, Cultural Studies Centre, University of Lagos, Akoka, Lagos, NIGERIA

Andrea Schlosshan, Saalburgstr. 75, 6000 Frankfurt a.M. 60, GERMANY

155

*Bernd Schulte*, Fachbereich Anglistik, Universität-GHS Siegen, 5900 Siegen, GERMANY

*Joachim Schultz*, Lehrstuhl für Romanische Literaturwissenschaft und Komparatistik, Universität Bayreuth, Postfach 101251, 8580 Bayreuth, GERMANY

*Omar Sougou*, B.P. 18-174 Pikine, Dakar, SÉNÉGAL.

*Peter O. Stummer*, Institut für Englische Philologie, Universität München, Schellingstr. 3, 8000 München 40, GERMANY

*Taban Lo Liyong*, Dept. of Education, University of Juba, PO Box, Khartoum, SUDAN

*Obiora Udechukwu*, c/o Boomerang Press, Friedrich-Puchta-Str. 26, 8580 Bayreuth, GERMANY

*Ahmed Yerima*, Dept. of English, Amadou Bello University, Zaria, NIGERIA

*Chantal Zabus*, Centre d'Enseignement et de Recherche en Etudes du Commonwealth, Université de Liège, 3 Place Cockerill, 4000 Liège, BELGIUM

Leonhard Harding/Brigitte Reinwald (Hg.)
AFRIKA – MUTTER UND MODELL DER EUROPÄISCHEN
ZIVILISATION
Die Rehabilitierung des schwarzen Kontinents durch Cheikh Anta Diop
287 Seiten
Broschiert DM 44,– / ISBN 3-496-00489-4

Der senegalesische Historiker Cheikh Anta Diop (1923 – 1986) ist einer der brillantesten
Wissenschaftler und aufregendsten »Querdenker« Afrikas. Er vertritt in seinen Werken
vehement die These, daß die ägyptische Kultur eine schwarzafrikanische Kultur gewesen
sei. Mit seinen Schriften, die hier erstmals in Auszügen in deutscher Übersetzung vor-
liegen, gibt Cheikh Anta Diop den Anstoß zu einer radikalen Revision der afrikanischen
und europäischen Geschichte.

Karl-Heinz Kohl/Heinzarnold Muszinski/Ivo Strecker (Hg.)
DIE VIELFALT DER KULTUR
Ethnologische Aspekte von Verwandtschaft, Kunst und Weltauffassung
(Mainzer Ethnologica, Band 4)
678 Seiten mit 23 Abbildungen
Leinen mit Schutzumschlag DM 138,– / ISBN 3-496-00388-X

Bei der Beschäftigung mit außereuropäischen Kulturen hat die Ethnologie Sichtweisen entwickelt, die sich auch bei der Untersuchung von Erscheinungsformen unserer eigenen
Zivilisation bewähren. Indem sie die Grenze zwischen »uns« und den »anderen« über-
windet, begreift sie die Unterschiede zwischen den Kulturen als Ausdruck der Vielfalt von
Kultur. Dieser Einsicht Ernst Wilhelm Müllers versuchen die Autoren dieses Bandes auf
den unterschiedlichsten Ebenen Rechnung zu tragen.

DIETRICH REIMER VERLAG  BERLIN
Unter den Eichen 57  ·  1000 Berlin 45

# DeBrosse, Redman, Black & Co., Ltd.

**Publishers**  Sandberry Press

CARIBBEAN POETRY SERIES
1. *Loggerhead* by Gloria Escoffrey
2. *A Tale from the Rainforest* by Edward Baugh
3. *Journey Poem* by Pamela Mordecai
4. *Strategies* by Dennis Scott
5. *Rain Carvers* by Judith Hamilton (forthcoming)

SUN RHYMES COLOURING BOOKS

**Booksellers and library jobbers specialising in Caribbeana**

**Suppliers of all media services**

P.O. Box 507
Kingston 10
809 927-6423

# GENÈVE-AFRIQUE - VOL. XXIX - N° 1 - 1991

**Conditions d'abonnement (2 numéros par année)**
FS 22.— + 4.— (port & emballage) = **FS 26.—**
**Prix du numéro: FS 15.—**

GENÈVE-AFRIQUE    -    Case postale 136    -    CH-1211 GENÈVE 21 - Suisse

# New titles from
# Hans Zell Publishers – 1991

## Reference

Shelagh Gastrow (ed.)
**Who's Who in South African Politics**
3rd fully revised and expanded edition
*384pp. 1991 £45.00/$85.00 cased*
*ISBN 0-905450-37-X*
(Co-published with Ravan Press)

A.H.M. Kirk-Greene (ed)
**A Biographical Dictionary of the British Colonial Service, 1939-1966**
*420pp. 1991 £85.00/$160.00 cased*
*ISBN 0-905450-96-5*

Cherry Gertzel
**Uganda: An Annotated Bibliography of Source Materials**
*244pp. 1991 £40.00/$75.00 cased*
*ISBN 0-905450-83-3*

Robert Collins
**The Waters of the Nile: An Annotated Bibliography**
*343pp. 1991 £55.00/$100.00 cased*
*ISBN 0-905450-84-1*

Carol Lems-Dworkin
**African Music: A Pan-African Annotated Bibliography**
*c.300pp. September 1991 c.£40.00/$75.00 cased*
*ISBN 0-905450-91-4*

G. F. Gorman & J. J. Mills
**Guide to Indexing and Abstracting Services in the Third World**
*c.220pp October 1991 c.£37.50/$70.00 cased*
*ISBN 0-905450-85-X*

Louis Taussig
**African Travel Resource Guide and Bibliography**
*c.360pp. December 1991 c.£49.50/$95.00 cased*
*ISBN 0-905450-77-9* (Guides to Travel Literature, 1)

## Monographs/Collections

Adebayo Adedeji, Sadig Rasheed, and Melody Morrison (eds.)
**The Human Dimension of Africa's Persistent Economic Crisis**
Selected Papers from the United Nations International Conference on the Human Dimension of Africa's Economic Recovery and Development, Khartoum, 5-8 March, 1988
*412pp. 1991 £44.00/$85.00 cased*
*ISBN 0-905450-40-X* (Published for the UN Economic Commission for Africa)

Austin N. Isamah
**Social Determinants of Labour Productivity in West Africa**
*189pp. 1991 £29.50/$55.00 cased*
*ISBN 0-905450-48-5* (ACARTSOD monograph series, African Social Challenges, 3)

ACARTSOD
**Social Development in Africa: Strategies, Policies and Programmes after the Lagos Plan**
*c.224pp. June 1991 £29.50/$55.00 cased*
*ISBN 0-905450-28-0* (ACARTSOD monograph series, African Social Challenges, 4)

Leonard Harris, Julia Maxted, and Abebe Zegeye (eds.)
**Exploitation and Exclusion: The Question of Race and Modern Capitalism**
*c.320pp. June 1991 £35.00/$65.00 cased*
*ISBN 0-905450-67-1*
(African Discourse series, 3)

Adrian Roscoe & Hangson Msiska
**The Quiet Chameleon: Modern Poetry from Central Africa**
*c.240pp. November 1991 c.£38.00/$70.00 cased*
*ISBN 0-905450-29-9* (New Perspectives on African Literature, 2)

**HANS ZELL PUBLISHERS**
**An imprint of Bowker-Saur Ltd.,**
**a Reed International Books Company**

*Orders to:*
Hans Zell Publishers, c/o Butterworth & Co. Publishers Ltd., Borough Green, Sevenoaks, Kent TN15 8PH, UK

*In the USA and Canada order from:*
Order Dept., K. G. Saur/R. R. Bowker, Post Office Box 31, New Providence, NJ 07974

*Editorial, and manuscript proposals:*
Hans Zell Publishers, PO Box 56, Oxford OX1 2SJ, UK

# THE INTERNATIONAL JOURNAL OF AFRICAN HISTORICAL STUDIES

*Norman R. Bennett, Editor*

*M. Jean Hay, Production Editor*

The International Journal of African Historical Studies, published quarterly, is devoted to the study of the African past. All aspects of Africa's history are covered, from prehistoric archaeology to the present problems of the continent, including the interaction between Africa and the Afro-American people of the New World. Articles are in both English and French, and the publication of original source materials, drawn from both written and oral sources, is encouraged. The book review section provides a thorough review of the current literature dealing with Africa's past.

Forthcoming in Volumes 23 (1990) and 24 (1991):
The Royal Women of Buganda, by Laurence Schiller; French Colonial Policy and the Family Life of Black Troops in French West Africa, 1828-1898, by Malcolm Thompson; Liberals and Local Administration in South Africa: The Alexandra Health Committee, 1933-1943, by David Duncan; East Coast Fever in Socio-Historical Context: A Case Study from Tanzania, by James Giblin; Race, Science, and the Legitimation of White Supremacy in South Africa, 1902-1940, by Paul Rich; British Commercial Policies Against Japanese Expansionism in East and West Africa, 1932-1935, by Kweku Ampiah; State, Ideology, and Power in Rhodesia, by Alan Cousins; The Horse in Fifteenth Century Senegambia, by Ivana Elbl; The Yoruba Caravan System of the Nineteenth Century, by Toyin Falola; Anaguta Revisited: An Essay in Historiographical Understanding, by Elizabeth Isichei; Women's History in South Africa, by Penelope Hetherington; and more!

Manuscripts and editorial correspondence should be sent to the Editor, International Journal of African Historical Studies, African Studies Center, Boston University, 270 Bay State Road, Boston, Massachusetts 02215 USA.

Subscription rates (per volume, published quarterly): $90.00 institutions and libraries, $30.00 individuals. Back-issue rates available on request. To subscribe, make checks payable in U.S. funds to IJAHS – African Studies Center, and send to IJAHS Subscriptions, African Studies Center, Boston University, 270 Bay State Road, Boston, Massachusetts 02215 USA.

available from:

**Boomerang-Press**

(Bummerang-Verlag)
Norbert Aas
A.-v.-Großstr.8
8580 Bayreuth

Germany

Obiora Udechukwu
**What the Madman Said**
Poems  &  Drawings

# GENÈVE-AFRIQUE - VOL. XXVIII - N° 2 - 1990

### Conditions d'abonnement (2 numéros par année)

Voie de surface:          FS 22.— +  4.— (port & emballage) = **FS 26.—**
Voie aérienne:          FS 22.— + 13.— (port & emballage) = **FS 35.—**

**Prix du numéro: FS 15.—**

GENÈVE-AFRIQUE    -    Case postale 136    -    CH-1211 GENÈVE 21 - Suisse

Volume XXII, no 2, Juin 1991

# ÉTUDES INTERNATIONALES

Directeur : Gérard HERVOUET.  
Directeur adjoint : Thierry HENTSCH.

Secrétaire de rédaction :  
Claude BASSET

## NUMÉRO SPÉCIAL

SOUS LA DIRECTION DE DANIEL C. BACH

# AFRIQUE :
## LA DÉCONNEXION PAR DÉFAUT

**CHRONIQUE DES RELATIONS EXTÉRIEURES DU CANADA ET DU QUÉBEC**

DIRECTION ET RÉDACTION : Centre québécois de relations internationales, Faculté des sciences sociales, Université Laval, Québec, Qué., Canada G1K 7P4, tél: (418) 656-2462, télécopieur : (418)656-3634.

SERVICE DES ABONNEMENTS : Les demandes d'abonnement, le paiement et toute correspondance relative à ce service doivent être adressés au Centre québécois de relations internationales, Faculté des sciences sociales, Université Laval, Québec, Qué., G1K 7P4, Canada.

ABONNEMENT ANNUEL :

Quatre numéros par an  
Régulier : $38.00 (Can.)  
Étudiant : $27.00 (Can.)  
Institution au Canada : $48.00 (Can.)

ÉTRANGER  
Régulier :$40.00 (Can.)  
Institution : $45.00 (Can.)  
le numéro: $16.00 (Can.)